HARCOURT SCHOOL PUBLISHERS

STORYtown

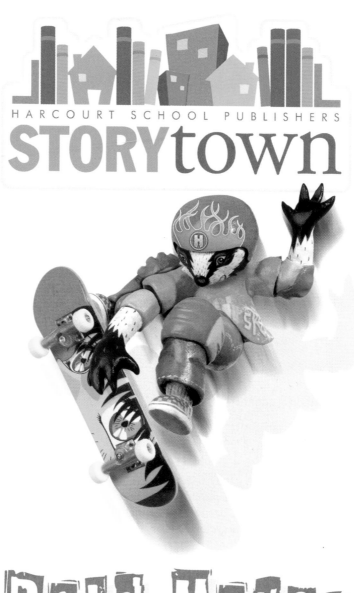

Bold Moves

Harcourt

SCHOOL PUBLISHERS

www.harcourtschool.com

Strategic Intervention Student Editions

Bold Moves, Grade 6

Copyright © by Harcourt, Inc.

Printed in the United States of America.

ISBN 0-15-354540-2
ISBN 978-0-15-354540-5

5 6 7 8 9 10 179 16 15 14 13 12 11 10 09

CONTENTS

CONTENTS

crestfallen

ecstatic

hysterical

incapacitated

lamented

mirth

perishable

ricocheted

Vocabulary

Build Robust Vocabulary

Write the Vocabulary Word that completes each sentence in the newspaper articles. The first one has been done for you.

DAILY NEWS   SECTION C

Comics to Compete in Class Act

by Zeke Gibson

Can you make kids giggle with

(1) _____ mirth _____?

Are they clutching their sides when

you make jokes? Think how sad

and **(2)** _____

they will be if you are not in the

Take-Two Class Act. Think how

(3) _____ they

will be to see you up at the mike. If you

have not added your name to the list, don't panic and get

(4) _____. You still have time to compete

for top comic. See Mr. Win to get your name on the list.

Class Act Still On

by Zeke Gibson

Ms. Moss will not be the critic for the acts this time. "She sipped some bad milk that made her sick," said Mr. Win. "**(5)**_____ goods like milk have dates on them. Ms. Moss said she'll look at the dates from now on." We can't have an **(6)**_____ critic, so Mr. Cutter will rate the acts.

Top prize this time is a ticket to see a live taping of the sitcom "Class Matters." "I wish we had time for lots of acts," **(7)** _____ Mr. Win. "In the past, one comic juggled apples as he cracked jokes. He missed one apple, which **(8)** _____ off a prop and hit me. That made me chuckle!"

The Comic

by Nick Pease
illustrated by Ilene Richard

June was hysterical. The Take-Two Class Act was happening, and she didn't have an act. Her chum Zeke was shocked at her plans.

"When did you get to be so brave?" he asked.

"Madison said it will be a blast," said June.

Stunned, Zeke said, "Did Madison state her plans?"

"No. . ." June said. "What's up?"

"Madison and Tom have a stand-up act!" said Zeke. "I think they asked you to do an act so they could win!"

June was crestfallen. "What a bad trick!" she sobbed. ❶

Stop and Think

❶ Why is Zeke surprised at June's plans?

Zeke is surprised because _____

_____

_____

"June," Zeke said with some misgiving. "The two of them joked that you were . . ."

"Dull!" June finished. "I *am* dull."

"Settle down!" said Zeke. "You are a bit timid, but you are not dull. You crack jokes all the time!"

"What made me think I could do this?" lamented June.

"You will be fine," Zeke said. "Take in some primetime TV, and snag some jokes. You could win this thing." ❷

Stop and Think

❷ How does June see herself? How does Zeke see her?

June sees herself as _____

Zeke sees June as _____

_____

Five sitcoms later, June still didn't have an act. And she was sick of so much TV.

But when she bumped into Madison and Tom, she acted like she was a comic whiz.

"How's your act shaping up, June?" asked Madison.

"It's topnotch," bragged June. "What a blast!"

"Madison and I will do a skit," Tom said, winking at Madison. "What will you do?"

"It's all hush-hush," said June. ❸

Stop and Think

❸ Why does June tell Madison and Tom that her act is "topnotch"?

June says her act is "topnotch" because _____

_____

_____

As the date for the act came closer, June was frantic. On the list of comics, someone had scribbled close to her name: "What a dud!"

"How can I compete with this?" June asked Zeke as she erased the crude note. "I can see kids chucking perishable crops at me, like rotten apples!"

"That will not happen," assured Zeke. "Besides, I don't think kids can bring apples." 4

Stop and Think

4 How would you feel if you were June? Explain.

I would feel _____

_____

_____

At last, it was time for the Take-Two Class Act to begin. June looked at her notes one last time. She could see the acts from her spot in the back. The fans liked some acts, and they clapped as some of them came to a close. June could see that Tom and Madison's skit was lame. Her classmates clapped just a little for them.

Then it was time for June's act. But as she went out in front of all her classmates, June panicked. She tripped over a box and toppled flat on her notes, scattering them all over. June's classmates began to shake with mirth at the incapacitated comic. June blushed and made a grab for the mike. ⑤

Stop and Think

⑤ What does June do on the stage?

On the stage, June _____

_____

_____

16

But the mike's pole pitched over and ricocheted off some props. Giggling classmates clutched their sides.

June sat up, stunned at what had happened. Without telling one joke, she was a comic hit!

Standing, June nodded to her fans and backed up, grasping the pole. She made some quick jabs with the pole and began to tap on her scattered notes. Gales of giggles rose from her fans. **6**

Stop and Think

6 What do you think will happen next?

I think June will _____

_____

_____

After her act, June was ecstatic. She could see that Tom and Madison were shocked. She was stunned when they came up to her and confessed, "We didn't think you could do it, but you were fantastic—a true comic hit!"

When the Take-Two Class Acts came to a close, June was voted the comic champ. As she strode out to take her prize, she could see her classmates smiling and clapping. And in the middle were Tom and Madison, now June's biggest fans.

Stop and Think

7 What do you think Tom and Madison learn?

I think they learn that _____

_____

_____

Think Critically

1. Do you think that Zeke is a good friend to June? Why do you think so? Use supporting details in your answer.
CHARACTER

I think that Zeke _____

_____

_____

2. How is June's problem solved? PLOT

Conflict

June is nervous about performing on stage.

Resolution

3. What do you learn from June about trying new things?
AUTHOR'S PURPOSE

I learn that _____

_____

_____

emerged

frolicked

hovered

inquire

meandering

subtle

survey

tormented

Vocabulary

Build Robust Vocabulary

Write the Vocabulary Word that completes each sentence. The first one has been done for you.

Tomás often watched the whales having fun as they jumped and **(1)** _____frolicked_____ in the sea. From the rocks, he could **(2)** _____ the beach and see the whales, too. Tomás liked to sing to them. He would step from one rock to the next as he sang each note.

One time, Tomás was **(3)** _____ along the rocks when he spotted an odd shape on the beach. It was a whale! A **(4)** _____ twitch of the whale's fin let Tomás know that it was alive.

Tomás looked out at the sea. Two whales **(5)** _____ from the waves and flapped their fins at Tomás. He thought, "That must be this whale's family!"

Tomás's sister Rosa was on the beach. She wanted to find out how the whale got there, but there was no time to **(6)** _____ about it. She ran to get help.

Tomás was **(7)** _____ by the whale's sad state. He **(8)** _____ over the whale, upset that he could not help it. "What can I do?" he said. "I must help this whale!"

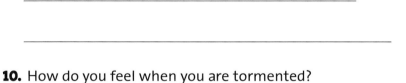

**Write the answers to these questions.
Use complete sentences.**

9. What do you do when you survey something?

_____

_____

10. How do you feel when you are tormented?

_____

_____

Song of the Sea

by Scott Light

illustrated by Lu Vazquez

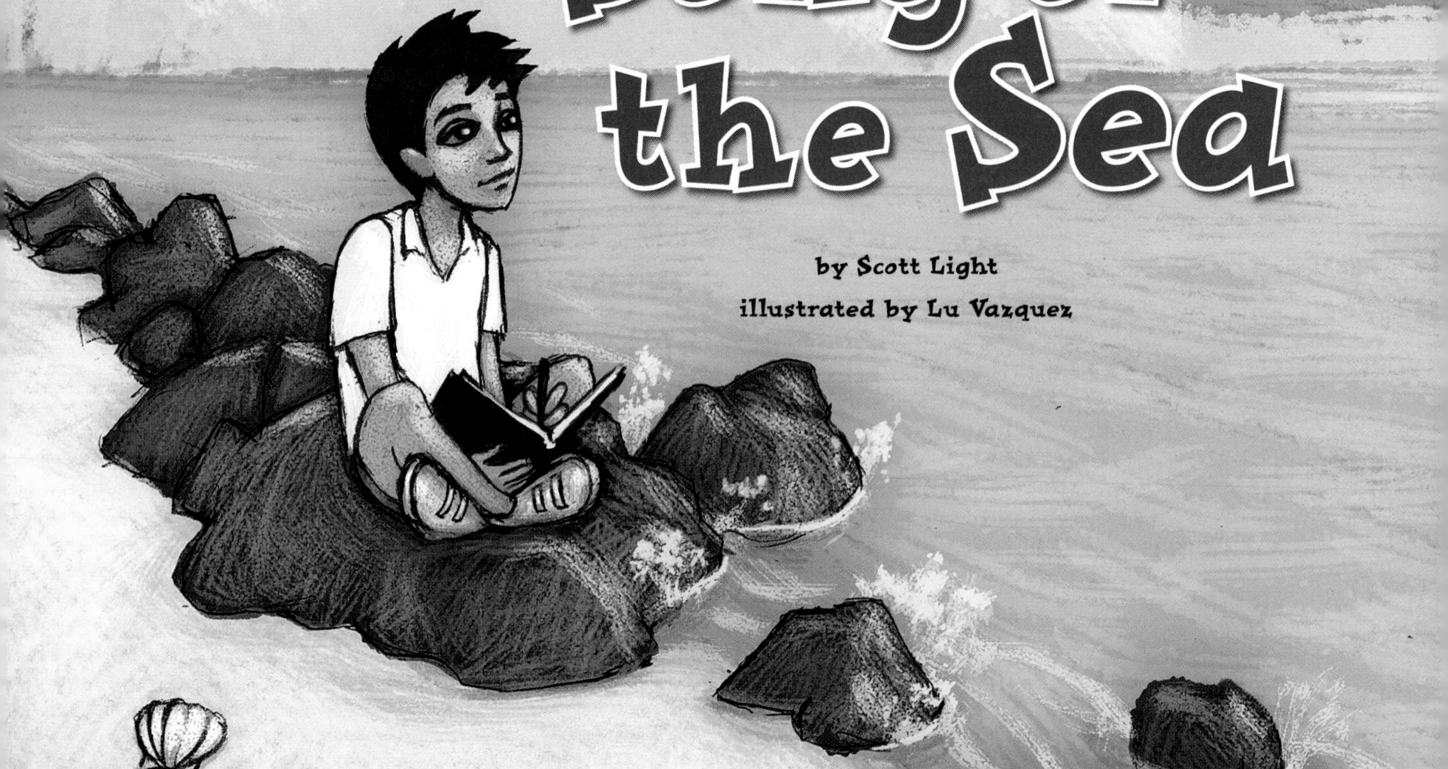

Every year, the whales
stopped in our cove on their
6,000-mile trip from the Bering Sea.
Many people would come from far-away
towns to see this amazing sight. They would
stand on the cliffs to survey the entire cove, filled with
whales. I, too, spent much of my time on the beach, but
for a different reason. ❶

Stop and Think

❶ What do you learn about the setting?

I learn that _____

_____

_____

You see, the beach was a great spot to write my songs. After I wrote them, I made them come to life. The whales seemed to like my singing, for they jumped and frolicked in the sea as my notes drifted over them.

Sometimes I wrote songs about the fish in the sea and the whales that ruled over them. I didn't care if the whales listened to me, as long as no one else did! My parents didn't know about my songs, but they had begun to inquire why I liked to spend so much time by myself.

Stop and Think

2 Why doesn't the narrator want anyone to hear his songs?

The narrator doesn't want anyone to hear his songs because

_____

_____

One day, I was meandering along the rocks when I spotted an odd shape on the beach. It was a whale! A whale on the beach was a bad thing, because whales needed to stay wet. Just as I headed for help, I spotted my sister Rosa walking toward me.

"Get help!" I yelled. "A whale is stuck on the beach!"

Rosa hovered for a second, then sped back down the beach. I stayed with the whale to keep watch. ③

Stop and Think

③ What is the problem in the story?

The problem is _____

_____

_____

In just minutes, my mom and dad were rushing down the beach, Rosa close on their heels.

"We need to get this whale back in the sea, and quick!" Dad said. "Tomás," he said, "you and Rosa keep the whale wet while we run and get help."

Rosa and I sat down next to the whale and began to splash water on it, wishing the tide would come in. ④

Stop and Think

④ What do you think will happen next?

I think that _____

_____

_____

The whale's look tormented me—it was trembling with fear, and I didn't see what else I could do to help it. Then I looked out at the other whales in the cove. They made me think of my songs and how much the whales liked them.

"I'll sing to it!" I said to Rosa.

"Sing? You?" Rosa looked at me, puzzled.

I began to sing, and the whale seemed to relax. A subtle twitch of its fin let me know that it was still alive. We kept splashing the whale as I sang my song. **5**

Stop and Think

5 What seems to make the whale relax?

The whale seems to relax when _____

_____

_____

26

Then, we heard a rumble of feet coming down the beach. My parents were back, and they were bringing help—lots of it, from what I could tell! It seemed as if the entire town had come to help save the whale.

I kept singing while everyone kept the whale wet. When the whale seemed to panic, I made my song softer to calm it down. **6**

Stop and Think

6 Think about what Tomás does. What can you tell about him?

I can tell that Tomás _____

_____

_____

At last the tide came in, and the whale drifted back out to sea. As it emerged in the cove, we all began to clap. But the clapping didn't stop when I did. With shock, I realized that they were now clapping for me!

"How did you make up those amazing songs?" asked my mom.

I described how I spent my time alone on the beach, and they were astonished.

"Keep writing your songs, Tomás," said my dad with pride. "But don't just sing them to the whales—we'd like to hear them, too!" **7**

Stop and Think

7 How do you think Tomás's life will be different now?

I think that _____

_____

_____

Think Critically

1. How is the problem in the story solved? Complete the story map with your answer. PLOT

Conflict
A whale is stuck on the beach.

Resolution

2. Why does the whale survive? CAUSE AND EFFECT

The whale survives because _____

_____

_____

3. What does this story tell you about sharing your talents? AUTHOR'S PURPOSE

This story tells me that _____

_____

_____

astounding

disbanded

exerts

replica

rigged

schemes

stabilize

Vocabulary

Build Robust Vocabulary

Read the selection and think about the meanings of the words in dark type.

Antonio López de Santa Anna was the president of Mexico between the years 1833 and 1855. After many losses in battle, Santa Anna's army **disbanded**, and he left his homeland. In the 1860s, he came to the United States hoping to get rich.

In New York, Santa Anna hired Tom Adams to be his assistant. Adams had attempted many money-making **schemes** but had not gotten rich yet. Adams told Santa Anna that he wanted to make strong tires and sell them. He was looking for an element to **stabilize** his tire mix. Santa Anna said that he could use *chicle*, a flexible sap from sapodilla trees in Mexico. Adams added *chicle* to his tires and **rigged** up a model. But when one **exerts** pressure on *chicle*, it will not keep its shape. The tire went flat.

Santa Anna helped Adams come up with an **astounding** product, but it wasn't a tire. You won't see their product on a **replica** of an old wagon. They made gum!

30

© Harcourt

Write answers to these questions. Use complete sentences.
The first one has been done for you.

1. What happens when an army is **disbanded**? Where do you think the men go?

   When an army is disbanded, they no longer go to

   battle. I think the men go home.

2. What are **schemes**? How can they help someone get rich?

   _____

   _____

3. Why did Adams need to **stabilize** the tire so someone could **exert** pressure on it?

   _____

   _____

4. Do you think that a **replica** of Adams's tire can be **rigged** up by anyone? Explain your answer.

   _____

   _____

5. What is the meaning of **astounding**? Name something that you think is astounding.

   _____

   _____

Tom Adams
and
Santa Anna

by Susan Blackaby

illustrated by C.B. Canga

Maps by Joe Le Monnier

Sometimes, an event happens that affects the lives of many. It could be a big event, such as inventing the plane, or it could be a small one. In this case, the event was small. But it resulted in something that you may take for granted.

Antonio López de Santa Anna was the president of Mexico between the years 1833 and 1855. Mexico was battling with the United States over land at the time. After many losses, Santa Anna's army disbanded, and he was asked to leave his homeland. In the 1860s, he came to America hoping to strike it rich. ❶

Stop and Think

❶ What do you want to learn from this selection?

I want to learn _____

_____

_____

Tom Adams was an American who had a gift for inventing things. He had attempted many money-making schemes but had not gotten rich yet. At the time Santa Anna arrived in New York, Adams was making tires. Adams was looking for the exact element to add to his tire mix. Everything he added just didn't work.

When Santa Anna landed on Staten Island, he hired Tom Adams to be his assistant. Adams let Santa Anna in on his plan for making tires. Santa Anna proposed a better plan that involved something from his homeland. ❷

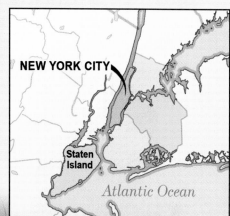

NEW YORK CITY

Staten Island

Atlantic Ocean

Stop and Think

❷ How are Tom Adams and Santa Anna alike? How are they different?

Here is how they are alike: _____

_____

Here is how they are different: _____

_____

Back in Mexico, people often munched on the milk-white sap from sapodilla trees. The sap, called *chicle* [CHIK•lay], was flexible like gum. Santa Anna said that he could get lots of *chicle*. In fact, he had taken some *chicle* with him to the United States after he was exiled, just in case he met someone who could use it.

Chicle has a lot of spring to it, and can be made into shapes. Santa Anna said that *chicle* could be added to the tires that Adams was making. He said he could get Adams a lot of *chicle*. If the plan was a hit, it could make them rich. ❸

Stop and Think

❸ **What do you think will happen next?**

I think that _____

_____

_____

Adams agreed to add *chicle* to his tires. For a small fee, Santa Anna had a big shipment of *chicle* sent to the United States.

Adams added the *chicle* to his tires. But when one exerts pressure on *chicle*, it will not keep its shape. It just stretches and stretches. This was not good at all. Adams attempted to stabilize the mixture by adding it to other things. He used the *chicle* in galoshes, in masks, and in balls. But for some reason, all of the things he made collapsed. The *chicle* was just too flexible. 4

Stop and Think

4 Why doesn't the *chicle* work?

It doesn't work because _____

_____

_____

For an entire year, Adams and his son attempted to use the *chicle*. But it sat in a heap, and Adams was all set to dump the shipment in the water of the East River. Then, he stopped in a sweet shop.

A kid was standing in line at the sweet shop, asking for a stick of gum. Gum! Adams recalled that *chicle* was used as gum in Mexico. In fact, Adams and his son had munched on the *chicle* themselves while making all those experiments. At last, Adams had a use for all of that *chicle*! **5**

Stop and Think

5 What happens after Adams decides to dump the *chicle*?

After he decides to dump the chicle, _____

_____

_____

Gum from tree resin was nothing new. People had been using it as gum for hundreds of years.

50 C.E. The Greeks use resin from the mastic tree as gum.

200 The Maya in South America use *chicle* as gum.

1600 Native Americans use tree resin as gum. The colonists use it, too, and sell lumps of it in shops.

1850 Paraffin wax is used to make gum.

1869 Adams uses *chicle* to make gum, just as the Mayans did.

1900 Gum is made in all shapes and sizes.

1928 Walter Diemer makes bubble gum.

Present There are over a thousand different gums for sale across the United States. ❻

Stop and Think

❻ What does the time line show?

The time line shows _____

_____

_____

In 1869, gum was made from wax. But *chicle* could stretch much better than wax. Adams and his son began selling small sticks of pure *chicle* gum. Ten years later, Adams rigged up some equipment to make the gum in bulk. People across the United States sampled the new gum. Its appeal was astounding! This brand of gum became a bestseller. Other gum makers began to make replicas of the new gum. Adams had struck it rich, and with some help from Santa Anna, kicked off the gum-making trade. ❼

Stop and Think

❼ Why do you think people like the new gum?

People like the new gum because _____

_____

_____

Think Critically

1. What did Tom Adams make after he gave up on tires?
Fill in the chart. SEQUENCE

> First, Adams tried using chicle to make tires.

> Next, Adams tried using chicle to make

> Finally, Adams made

2. How did Santa Anna help Tom Adams? MAIN IDEA AND DETAILS

Santa Anna helped Tom Adams by _____

_____

_____

3. What words might describe Tom Adams? CHARACTER

Tom Adams was _____

_____

_____

astonishment

fumble

intense

lunged

luxury

propel

remedies

triumphant

Vocabulary

Build Robust Vocabulary

Write the Vocabulary Word that completes each sentence in the advertisements. The first one has been done for you.

See Babe on the Track!

What is one of the best

(1) _____remedies_____

for the blahs? Watch with

(2) _____ as

Babe Didrikson sprints to a win!

The $2 fee makes this event a

(3) _____ you

do not have to pass up!

Play Ball, Babe!

Come and see Babe in a softball

game! She can tag the other team out

with ease. At the last game, Babe

(4) _____ to make an

out at home plate. Get set to cheer her next

(5) _____ win!

© Harcourt

40

Babe at Basketball

Babe is a whiz at basketball. At all of the games, she leads her team to the top. You will not see Babe make a

(6) _____

by dropping the ball. Do not miss this week's game!

Babe on the Links

Fans say that no one can

(7) _____

a golf ball like Babe can! She can hit the ball as far as 250 yards. Even under

(8) _____

pressure, Babe can make a hole-in-one.

Babe
in the Hall of Fame

by Susan Blackaby

When Mildred Didrikson was a kid, she was a baseball whiz. In one game, she hit five home runs! Some of her teammates started calling her Babe for Babe Ruth, the baseball star. The nickname stuck. And Babe Didrikson went on to become one of the top athletes of all time.

Babe was born in Texas in 1911, one of seven children. Times were hard. Her dad didn't make much money. All of the Didrikson children liked competing in sports. But Babe liked competing in *all* sports. **1**

Babe, 18, tosses a discus at a track event.

Stop and Think

1 What do you think you will learn in this selection?

I think I will learn _____

_____

_____

As a teen, Babe was the best at basketball.

Babe liked to win. When she dribbled a basketball, she didn't make a fumble. In a game of softball, she lunged so that she might make the out at home plate. She could hit a tennis ball as well as she could pitch a strike.

But Babe had a real fondness for basketball. As a teen, she was the best on her team. In 1930, the owner of a basketball team watched Babe in a game and asked her to play on his team. In 1932, the team won the U.S. championship game. Babe was the spark that led the team to this top spot. Seeing her talent in track, the team's owner started a track team, too. ➋

Stop and Think

➋ What made the team owner start a track team?

The owner started a track team because _____

_____

_____

BORN

OLYMPICS
(track and field)

When it came to track events, Babe was in a class all by herself. She ran and jumped like a deer. Her arm was so strong that she could propel a javelin for what seemed like miles. No one came close to doing what Babe could do. She won many medals at track events in 1932.

During those times, a woman athlete couldn't earn money from competing in sports like men did. These athletes were seen as "odd ducks." Many people asked, "Why do they want to act like men?" **3**

Stop and Think

3 How were women athletes treated in the 1930s?

In the 1930s, women athletes were treated _____

_____

_____

©Harcourt

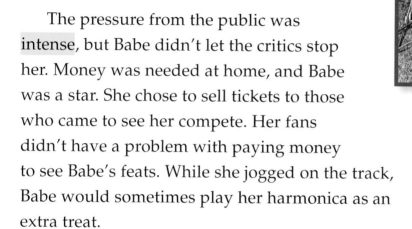

1935	1940	1953	1956
GOLF	PRO GOLF	ILL	DIES

The pressure from the public was intense, but Babe didn't let the critics stop her. Money was needed at home, and Babe was a star. She chose to sell tickets to those who came to see her compete. Her fans didn't have a problem with paying money to see Babe's feats. While she jogged on the track, Babe would sometimes play her harmonica as an extra treat.

At that time, taking part in sports was a luxury for women. Women athletes were barred from competing in most sports. But golf wasn't off limits. Starting in the 1930s, Babe set out to make her mark in golf. Babe spent much of her time hitting golf balls. She struck up to fourteen thousand balls a week! **4**

Stop and Think

4 Think about Babe's actions. What can you tell about her?

I can tell that Babe _____

_____

_____

Just as you might predict, Babe was remarkable. When she smacked the ball, it went off like a rocket! She was asked how she could get a golf ball to go 250 yards in one stroke. Babe gave a quick-witted response. She said, "You've got to . . . let it rip!"

For a while, a woman athlete couldn't earn money playing golf. So Babe helped start a golf club for women so that they could compete for money. Babe kept up her triumphant winning streak as she kept on golfing at the start of the 1950s. **5**

Stop and Think

5 Think about the problems Babe faced. How would you feel if you were Babe? Explain your answer.

I would feel _____

_____

_____

© Harcourt

In 1953, Babe got sick. It seemed like the end of golf for her. But to the astonishment of all, Babe was back at the game in no time. She had five wins in 1954. Her game didn't appear to be harmed. People called her the "comeback kid."

But there were no remedies for the disease that Babe had. She lost the battle with her sickness in the fall of 1955. **6**

Babe blasts the ball out of a sand trap at a 1953 golf contest.

Stop and Think

6 What happened to Babe in 1953?

In 1953, _____

_____

_____

The press named Babe Didrikson a top athlete of the 1900s. She was inducted into the halls of fame for both track and golf. Some still think that she is one of the best athletes of all time.

Babe's career was a triumphant one. As a gifted athlete, she helped to change the face of sports for women. From start to finish, Babe was a hall-of-fame star. **7**

Babe poses with the top prize from the 1947 Women's British Amateur Golf Championship in Scotland.

Stop and Think

7 How did Babe help women today?

Babe helped women today by _____

_____

_____

©Harcourt

Think Critically

1. What sports did Babe play in her lifetime? Fill in the graphic organizer. SEQUENCE

> **First**
> *Babe played softball and tennis.*

> **Next**
> *Babe played basketball.*

> **Then**

> **Finally**

2. How did Babe solve the problems she faced?
   MAIN IDEA AND DETAILS

   Babe solved the problems by _____

   _____

3. Why is it important to learn about Babe Didrikson?
   AUTHOR'S PURPOSE

   It's important because _____

   _____

Vocabulary

Build Robust Vocabulary

Write the Vocabulary Word that best completes each sentence. The first one has been done for you.

1. Kendall was afraid. It's _____intimidating_____ to meet

   steadfast   perishable   intimidating

   a big pop star like Kara.

2. She bit her nails. She was filled with

   _____.

   composure   trepidation   mirth

3. Chris looked sick. His fear _____

   disbanded   surpassed   lunged

   Kendall's.

4. Chris hoped there would be no _____

   calamity   composure   remedy

   on the set.

5. The two were in a _____.

          replica   quandary   luxury

They had to calm themselves.

6. They wanted to be good hosts, but fear can be a

_____.

hindrance   remedy   scheme

7. Their teacher gave them a _____

         crestfallen   tormented   sage

bit of wisdom.

8. This _____ bit of wisdom helped

invaluable   incapacitated   intimidating

them calm down.

9. They decided to be _____ and

       perishable   steadfast   hysterical

stick with the plan.

10. They felt calm after they regained their

_____.

astonishment   composure   calamity

Write the answers to these questions. Use complete sentences.

11. What makes you feel trepidation?

_____

_____

12. What do you have that is invaluable to you?

_____

_____

My Song

BY MICHELLE KIRBY

ILLUSTRATED BY DAVE GORDON

CHARACTERS

- **NARRATOR**
- **CHRIS**, HOST
- **KENDALL**, HOST
- **MUSIC TEACHER**
- **KARA CLARK**, SINGER
- **CHORUS**

NARRATOR: The sixth grade class is all set to greet pop singing star Kara Clark. The class is buzzing with glee as the students wait for her to arrive. Hosts Chris and Kendall look afraid and tense.

CHRIS: Will you stop biting your nails, Kendall?

KENDALL: It's intimidating to meet a big star like Kara.

CHRIS: I'm with you there! I just hope she likes us. ❶

Stop and Think

❶ How do Chris and Kendall feel? How do their classmates feel?

Chris and Kendall feel _____

Their classmates feel _____

© Harcourt

52

NARRATOR: Kendall plops down on her hands to keep from biting her nails, while Chris fiddles with his pen.

MUSIC TEACHER: Chris, Kendall, are you two all set?

KENDALL: I think we are, if Chris can stay calm.

MUSIC TEACHER: Chris, how are you? You do look a bit sick.

CHRIS: I *am* just a little bit scared, but I'm eager to get started. I hope we don't set off a calamity on the set!

MUSIC TEACHER: Don't fear—you two will be a big hit with the famed Kara. Have some faith in yourselves, for that's the key to doing a fine job. ②

Stop and Think

② What challenge do Chris and Kendall face?

Their challenge is _____

_____

_____

NARRATOR: Chris and Kendall take their seats on the set, and the rest of the class sits down. Chris's hands start to shake, but he regains his composure as he begins to speak.

CHRIS: I'm Chris Kane along with Kendall Hanley. We have a treat for you today on Sixth Grade Live! We'll be talking to the fantastic and talented Kara Clark. We begged and pleaded and . . . she's agreed to sing for us!

KENDALL: Kara just walked away with two Top Pop prizes for best artist and best song.

CHRIS: We won't keep you waiting, so bring her out! ③

Stop and Think

③ Would you be nervous if you were Chris? Explain.

I would _____

_____

_____

NARRATOR: The class stands and claps as Kara Clark walks on the set. Kara smiles and waves, then she sits down and looks at the hosts.

KENDALL: We're so glad you agreed to talk with us today.

KARA CLARK: It's always nice to meet and chat with fans.

CHRIS: Speaking of Kara buffs, do they send much fan mail?

KARA CLARK: I get up to six hundred notes a week!

CHORUS: Oh my, that's a lot of mail!

CHRIS: Do you respond to all of them?

KARA CLARK: It's nice to get so much mail, but it's a quandary. I want to respond to all of them, but I just don't have the time. ❹

Stop and Think

❹ What happens after Kara Clark walks on stage?

After Kara walks on stage, _____

_____

_____

KENDALL: How did you get involved in the frantic life of singing?

KARA CLARK: I started singing when I was just ten. I wanted to tag along with my big sis when she started singing lessons, and I liked making tunes from the start.

CHRIS: Did you always like singing in public?

KARA CLARK: No way! I was afraid a lot of the time. For years I felt such trepidation each time I had to go out and sing in public. One time, my costume snagged on the stands, and I landed on the spectators in the middle of a song. It was so embarrassing!

CHORUS: No way!

CHRIS: We had no idea that things were so difficult for you. You have such composure that it's hard to think that you were afraid. How did you get past the fear? ❺

Stop and Think

❺ What problem did Kara face when she first started singing?

Kara _____

_____

_____

KARA CLARK: I wanted to sing, and it was a big hindrance to be afraid. I couldn't let my fear get in the way of my dream, so I had to be strong and just keep singing. It was hard, but I had a fantastic teacher who helped me.

CHRIS: In what ways did this teacher help?

KARA CLARK: He gave me this sage bit of wisdom: pretend you are singing your song alone and always have fun. Simple, but his invaluable lessons helped me get to be who I am today.

CHORUS: Simple, yet so wise!

KENDALL: Do you have some inspiring tips for someone hoping to be a star someday? 6

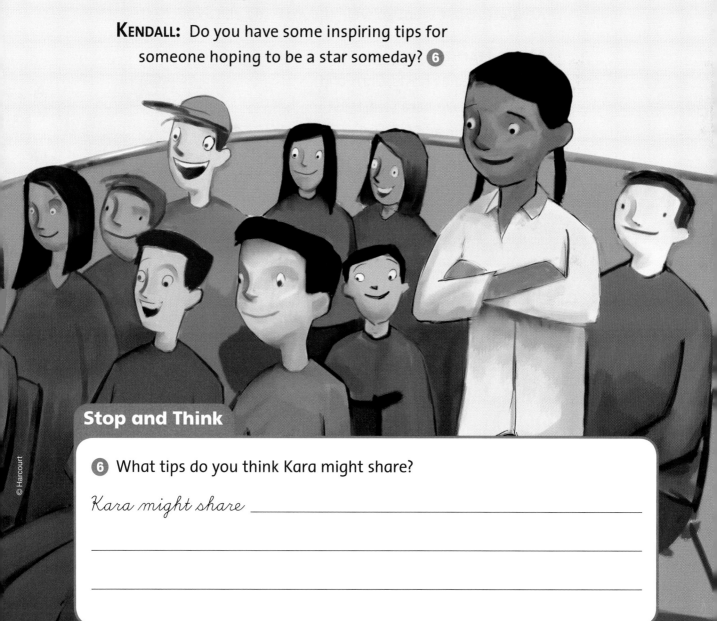

Stop and Think

6 What tips do you think Kara might share?

Kara might share _____

_____

_____

KARA CLARK: All you can do is be steadfast and stick with it. When you're afraid and it seems like your dream won't happen, just keep at it. Don't give up if you do strike out. It may take time to get where you want to go.

CHRIS: Sage wisdom indeed, and that's all the time we have. Let's end with Kara Clark singing her chart-topping song, "Bring on the Rain."

NARRATOR: Kara Clark belts out her song as thrilled fans jump up and begin clapping, singing, and swaying. Then she salutes the class with a wave, and leaves.

KENDALL: That went so well! It surpassed all I expected!

MUSIC TEACHER: I'm pleased with how you acted as hosts, Chris and Kendall. Like Kara said, trust in yourself, and you can go a long way. **7**

Stop and Think

7 What do the hosts learn about overcoming fears?

They learn that _____

_____

_____

Think Critically

1. Do you think Chris and Kendall were good hosts? Explain. **CHARACTERS**

I think that Chris and Kendall _____

_____

_____

2. How do you think Chris and Kendall felt at the end? **PLOT**

I think they felt _____

_____

_____

3. Think about how Kara felt when she first started singing. Then think about how Chris and Kendall felt before the interview. How were their experiences alike? **COMPARE AND CONTRAST**

Kara, Chris, and Kendall all _____

_____

fused

haywire

immobile

intonation

jest

sinuous

supple

Vocabulary

Build Robust Vocabulary

Write the Vocabulary Word that completes each sentence in the diary. The first one has been done for you.

Monday

Things in Ms. Kim's class went **(1)** _____haywire_____ from the second the bell went off. This week is Teamwork Week. My teammate is a new kid, Wendell. I don't know him at all!

We have to make models. I hate making models! And I am not saying this in **(2)** _____. I mean it. We'll have to get a lot of little parts to make something big. Then who knows if it will work when the parts are all

(3) _____ into one.

Tuesday

Yesterday, I met with Wendell to work on our project. I think we have a plan for the model! At first, I just sat there. I was as

(4) _____ as a bump on a log. I didn't think I could help at all. But then Wendell said in just the right

(5) _____, "You can do it, Carla! Let's think of a plan!"

I came up with the plan, and it includes working with clay. Clay is very soft and **(6)** _____. I had fun twisting it into a long and **(7)** _____ snake. It looks so real, the kids in class may be afraid of it! Maybe I'll take out the snake. I can't wait to work on the model again!

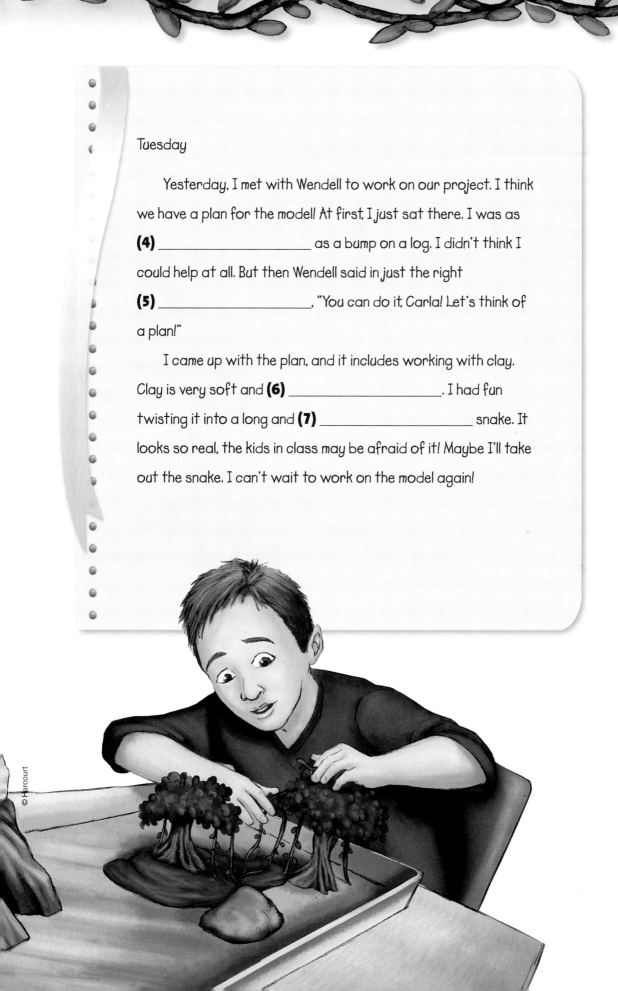

It Takes Two!

by Judy Giglio

illustrated by Todd Kale

Sitting at her desk, Carla scanned the line of classmates as they filed in to take their seats.

"What happened to you?" she asked a dripping Ben as he shuffled into class, his soaked loafers squeaking as he passed by.

"I was waiting at the bus stop when this over-sized truck came sailing down the hill and splashed me!" he exclaimed.

"Looks like you and the truck started the day on a downhill slope," Carla said in jest. ❶

Stop and Think

❶ Do you think Ben is upset? Why do you think so?

I think that Ben _____

_____

_____

"This week is Teamwork Week," said Ms. Kim. "You will team up with a classmate, and your goal will be to use your talents to make a model for some new object."

Carla was thinking she would ask Ben. They would make a good team.

"I'll pull out two names at a time from this box," Ms. Kim explained. "The names I pick will be teammates."

Carla sat immobile as Ms. Kim called out names.

"Carla Vargas . . . and Wendell Oaks," finished Ms. Kim.

"Oh, no," Carla said to herself. "I don't know him!" **2**

Stop and Think

2 What problem does Carla face?

Carla's problem is _____

_____

_____

After class, a reluctant Carla agreed to meet Wendell after school to work on their project.

Later, at Wendell's home, Mrs. Oaks greeted Carla and invited her to come inside. "Wendall is down in his lab," she explained.

Lab? Just what am I getting into now? Carla wondered as she stepped down the dark stairs.

In the basement, Wendell had just finished working on a model car. ❸

Stop and Think

❸ Do you think Wendell will be a good teammate? Explain.

I think that Wendell _____

_____

_____

"Do you like to make models?" Carla asked.

"I sure do," Wendell said, adding, "Do you?"

"I'm not good at making models," Carla admitted, thinking of the model boat she made last year that floated for a few seconds. "They just go haywire."

"Come on, Carla!" coaxed Wendell. "It takes two to make a team, and I'm sure you have a talent to add."

"Well, I *am* best at planning things," offered Carla. "What if we make a model for an amusement park ride?"

"Yes—fantastic!" Wendell agreed. "Let's make it a floating boat ride."

"Ummm, sure," Carla said, her intonation indicating just how unsure she was. ❹

Stop and Think

❹ What can you tell about Carla?

I can tell that Carla _____

_____

_____

Carla let Wendell coach her as they looked for parts they could use. Carla was amazed at the way Wendell could twist clay shapes for tree trunks and add snake-like sinuous vines hanging down. Carla used the soft, supple clay to make a cave for the boat ride.

They put the model in a pan filled with water to make a moat around the tree grove. Small boats were made from foam trays and set on foam balls to keep them afloat. Wendell linked the boats with string. **5**

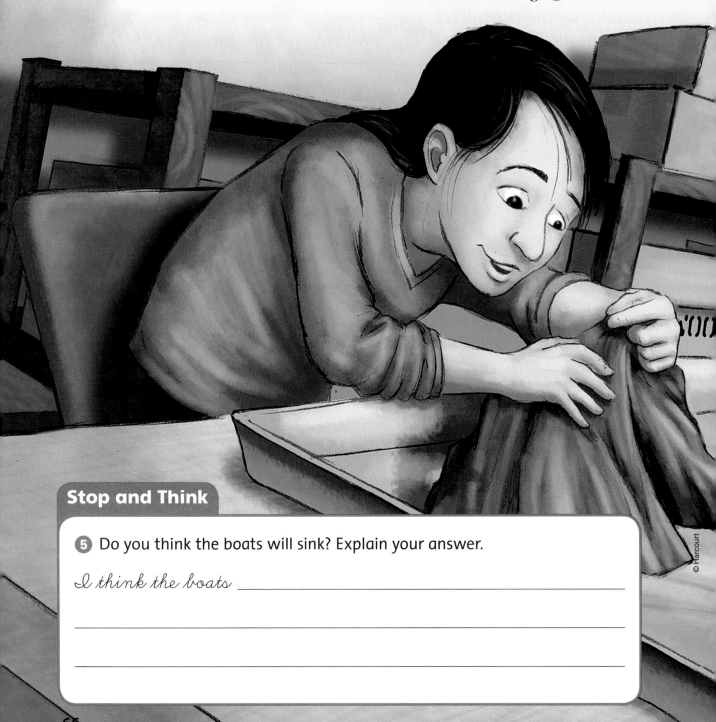

Stop and Think

5 Do you think the boats will sink? Explain your answer.

I think the boats _____

_____

_____

66

"Wendell is an artist, a brain, and a good teammate all fused into one," Carla nodded to herself.

When the model was done, the boats went around the moat and floated in and out of the cave.

"We did it!" Carla exclaimed, as Wendell sat back and admired the model.

"Let's make a tape of water bubbling and running, like in a stream," Carla said. "We can play it while we present the speech to make it realistic."

"Good plan!" agreed Wendell, grabbing a tape. **6**

OLD BOOK

SUPER MOVERS

Stop and Think

6 How does Carla feel about having Wendell as a teammate now?

Carla feels _____

_____

_____

© Harcourt

67

In class, Wendell clicked on the water tape and glided the boats around as Carla spoke. Wendell's hands and the tape of bubbling water made the model come to life.

After the speech, Carla and Wendell let their amazed classmates see the model up close.

"How did you do this?" Ben exclaimed. "After last year's boat flop, I didn't think you could make a thing!"

"Carla planned it all," Wendell boasted.

"Well, Wendell made the plan work," Carla insisted. "Without him, the boats would have sunk like stones!" **7**

Stop and Think

7 How do Carla and Wendell use different talents to work together?

Carla _____

_____

Wendell _____

_____

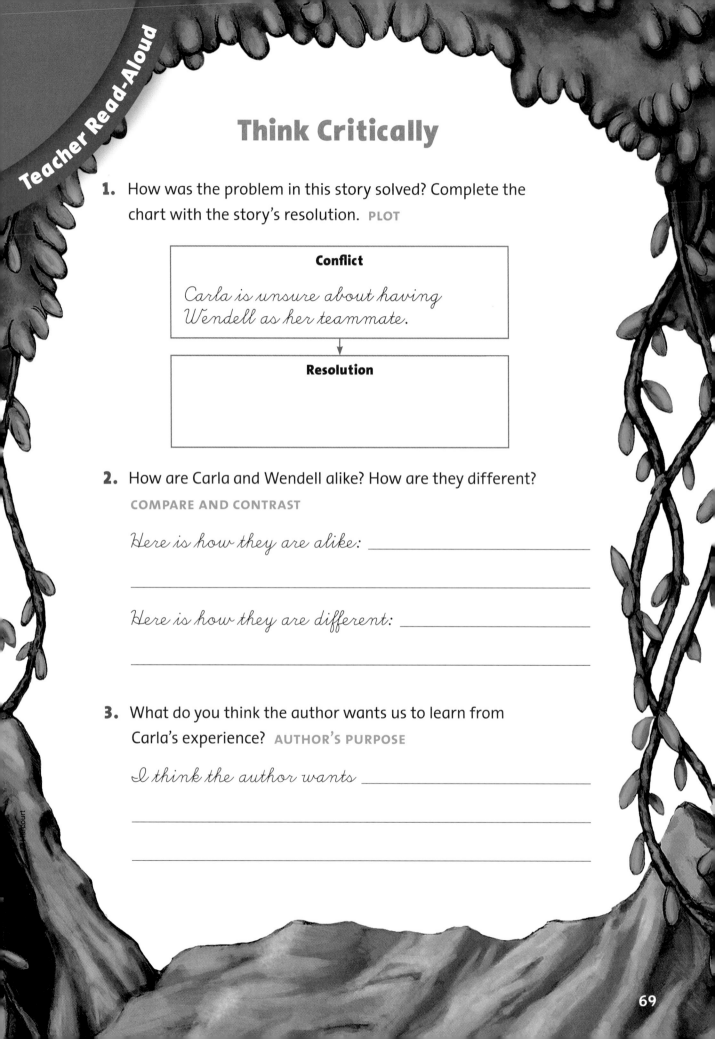

Think Critically

1. How was the problem in this story solved? Complete the chart with the story's resolution. **PLOT**

> **Conflict**
>
> Carla is unsure about having Wendell as her teammate.

↓

> **Resolution**
>
>

2. How are Carla and Wendell alike? How are they different? **COMPARE AND CONTRAST**

Here is how they are alike: _____

_____

Here is how they are different: _____

_____

3. What do you think the author wants us to learn from Carla's experience? **AUTHOR'S PURPOSE**

I think the author wants _____

_____

_____

convince

defeatist

disown

ordinary

rejected

suit

treason

Vocabulary

Build Robust Vocabulary

Write the Vocabulary Word that completes each sentence. The first one has been done for you.

"Gail, you sing so well," Mom said. She wanted to

(1) _____convince_____ Gail to sing with the Harlem

Stars Glee Club.

The Harlem Stars had always been all male, but now

females could be part of the show. Some would think

the Harlem stars were committing (2) _____

if they let females sing with them.

Yesterday, Mr. Willow had asked Gail to sing with them.

She had (3) _____ his request, saying,

"I don't think I can sing like them."

Gail didn't think their style of singing would

(4) _____ her. Her style of singing

was very different from theirs.

© Harcourt

70

Gail said she didn't think she could do it. Her mom didn't like her **(5)** _____ attitude.

In bed, Gail couldn't sleep. She was thinking, *My mom and dad would* **(6)** _____ *me if I didn't take the risk.* Gail had always had a close bond with her parents. She wanted it to stay that way.

The next day, Gail said she was going to sing with the Harlem Stars. Her mom was all smiles as she said, "You're no **(7)** _____ kid, Gail." Gail's mom was impressed.

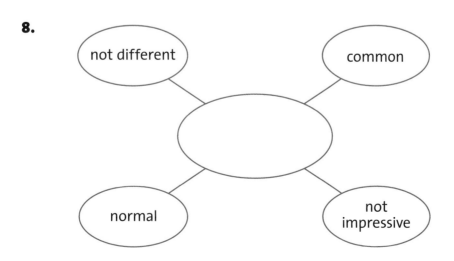

Write the Vocabulary Word that best completes the synonym web.

8.

- not different
- common
- normal
- not impressive

The Mixed-Up All-Stars

by Judy Giglio

illustrated by Aaron Jasinski

"You can't convince me to do it," I said to my mom. I gazed out the window to hide my feelings.

"But Gail, you sing so well. I'd be so sad to see you waste a talent like yours," she said.

"So you like my crowing?" I joked, smiling.

"You sing!" Mom was quick to respond. "You do *not* crow. Honey, just assure me that you won't pass up things like this that can help you grow as an artist."

"Well, let me sleep on it," I said. **1**

Stop and Think

1 What does Gail mean when she says she'll "sleep on it"?

Gail means that _____

_____

_____

72

The best showcase around for singing had always been the Harlem Stars Glee Club. They were all male, but now females could be part of the show. Yesterday, Mr. Willow asked Deb, Marisa, and me to join the club. He said he wanted to see if his idea would work.

At first, I rejected his request. I didn't think their style would suit me. The Harlem Stars tend to sing low notes with a slow beat. My talent was singing high notes with a fast beat. I didn't think my singing would blend in with theirs at all. And some would think the Harlem Stars were committing treason if they let females sing with them anyway. **2**

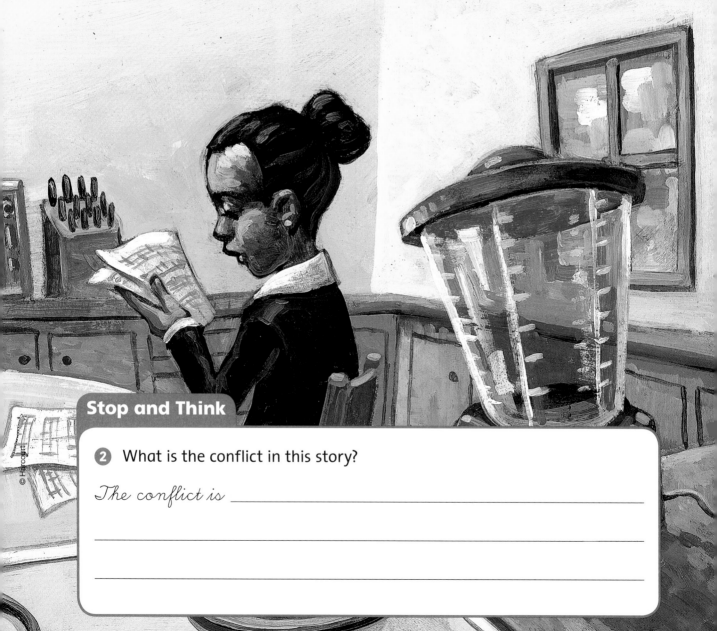

Stop and Think

2 What is the conflict in this story?

The conflict is _____

_____

_____

The next morning, I looked out my window and could see that the remaining snow had melted. Small green buds had started to grow on the trees. I felt that maybe it was time for me to grow, too.

"Mom, I'm going to sing with the Harlem Stars," I said as I grabbed a waffle out of the toaster. "I think that I need to at least see if this will work."

My mom was all smiles. She held my hands in hers. "You're no ordinary kid, Gail. I know you can do this. And we won't disown you if it doesn't work out."

Later in class, Mr. Willow explained that the Harlem Stars would now be called the Harlem All-Stars! We were thrilled to be a part of this new group. ③

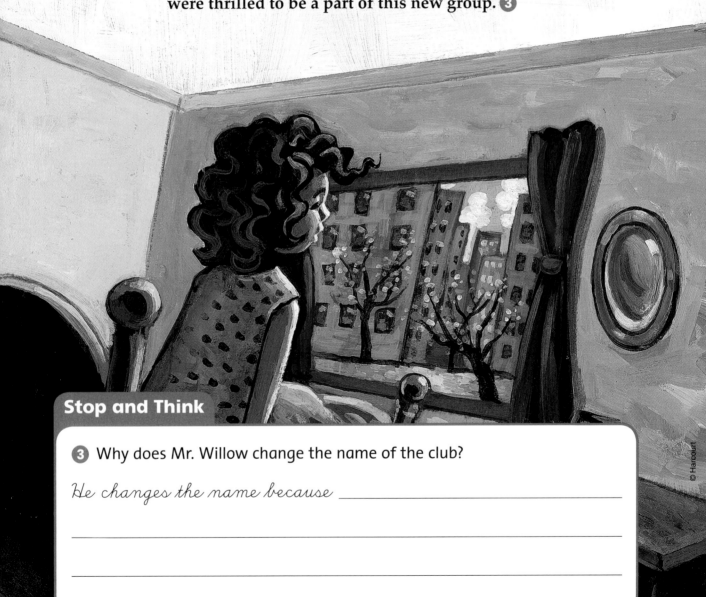

Stop and Think

③ Why does Mr. Willow change the name of the club?

He changes the name because _____

_____

_____

We soon realized that singing with the Harlem All-Stars was going to be hard. All the songs had been chosen for males. Some songs were upbeat, but not one of them had parts for high voices. They were all low, slow, and mellow. I began to wonder if this jumble of voices would make people start calling the group the Mixed-Up All-Stars.

"I think this is a mistake," I said to Dad after school. "There are no parts in their songs for our high voices. When all of us sing together, our voices clash like pots and pans."

"That's a defeatist attitude, Gail," Dad declared. "Don't give up. Find a way to show what you can do." **4**

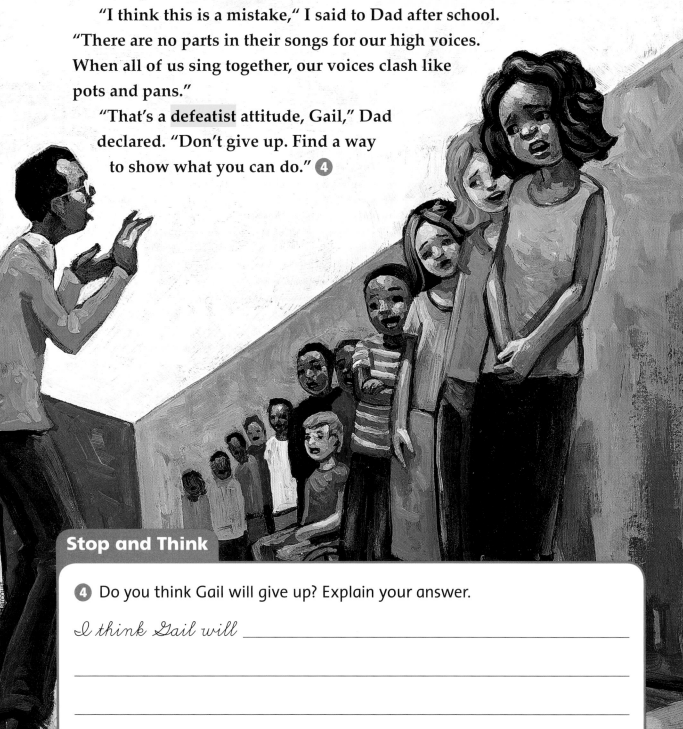

Stop and Think

4 Do you think Gail will give up? Explain your answer.

I think Gail will _____

_____

_____

That night, my dad's lesson repeated over and over in my mind until I drifted off to sleep. I dreamed the new Harlem All-Stars were singing their low, slow notes when Deb, Marisa, and I walked out. I started singing in my high voice, and the beat picked up speed. Then Deb and Marisa chimed in. Our part of the song was all new. The entire group sang with a crisp, clear beat, and our voices began to blend together at last. **5**

Stop and Think

5 What is happening in Gail's dream?

In Gail's dream, _____

_____

_____

© Harcourt

When I woke up, that new part to the song was still fresh in my mind. I rushed to find Marisa and Deb and sang the new part the same way I had sung it in my dream. Marisa and Deb followed my lead, and our pleasing notes drifted down the hall. Now, we realized, we had to show Mr. Willow and the rest of the Harlem All-Stars what we wanted to do. But, would they agree?

When we demonstrated our plan, Mr. Willow and the Harlem All-Stars stopped and smiled. Mr. Willow said that he had been thinking about how to get our voices to blend better, too. They all agreed that adding this new part to the song would blend our high voices with their own low ones. **6**

Stop and Think

6 How do you think the girls feel now? Why do you think so?

I think the girls feel _____

_____

_____

In just two weeks, we were ready for our first Harlem All-Stars show.

As we started to sing, I watched the effect we were having on the people listening. Some smiled and leaned toward us, as if they wanted to hear more. Some nodded with the beat. They all seemed to like the way our high and low voices blended. Best of all, when the show ended they wouldn't stop clapping. We were not mixed-up after all! We had become the Harlem All-Stars. ❼

Stop and Think

❼ What do you learn about sharing talents?

I learn that _____

_____

_____

Think Critically

1. How was the conflict in this story resolved? Write the plot events in the story map. **PLOT**

Conflict
Gail doesn't want to sing in the Club.

Plot Events
1. *Gail's mom urges Gail to sing.*
2.
3.
4.

Resolution
The All-Stars are a hit.

2. Why does the author describe Gail's dream? **AUTHOR'S PURPOSE**

The author describes Gail's dream because _____

_____

_____

3. Why does Gail decide to try out for the Harlem Stars Glee Club? **CHARACTERS**

Gail decides to try out because _____

_____

_____

devoured

diagnosed

intercept

lethal

plea

rendezvous

seeped

Vocabulary

Build Robust Vocabulary

Read the selection and think about the meanings of the words in dark type.

In 1918, doctors were seeing a new form of disease. Back then, they were just starting to understand diseases. With scopes, they could look at small organisms. They could watch as one organism **devoured** another.

The new disease baffled doctors. As it passed from man to man, the disease gained strength. In no time at all, it was **lethal**. In just one month, the disease claimed 12,000 lives. Doctors **diagnosed** it and called it the Spanish Flu.

At an army camp in Boston, doctors sent out a **plea** for help. A doctor named Victor Vaughan was the one to **intercept** the call. He went to Boston and found that hundreds were sick.

The disease seemed to follow the railroads, and at each railway **rendezvous** point, the disease was passed. Many strapped on masks to keep from getting sick, but the organism **seeped** into the masks' small holes. The health of the entire United States was at risk.

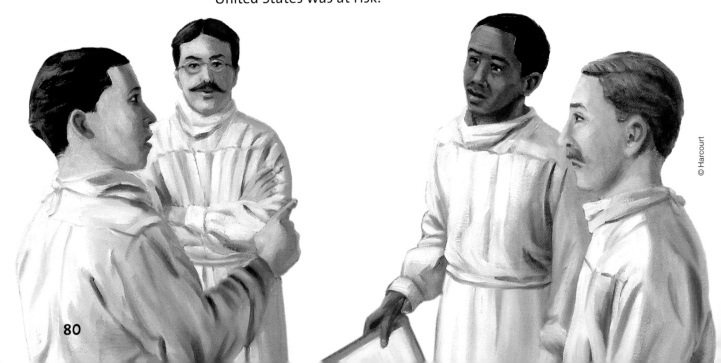

© Harcourt

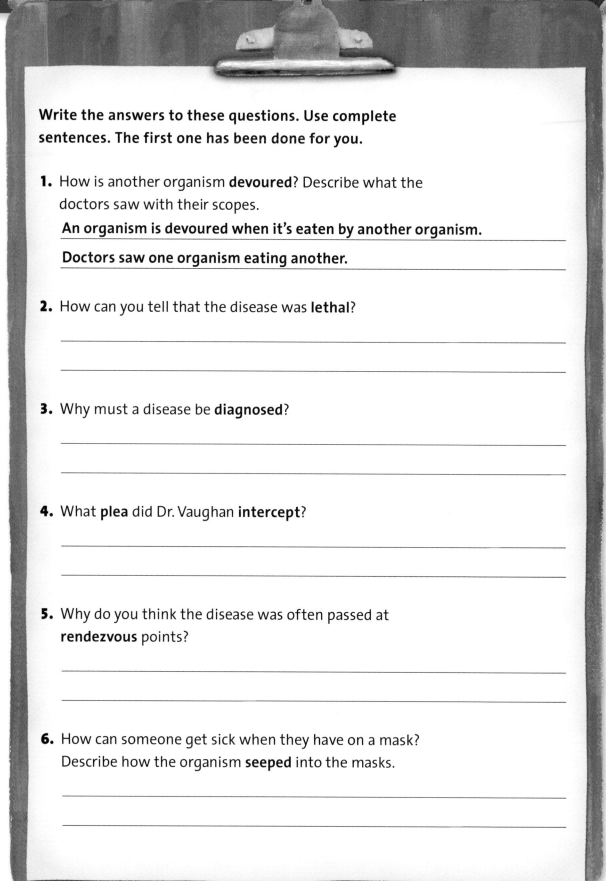

Write the answers to these questions. Use complete sentences. The first one has been done for you.

1. How is another organism **devoured**? Describe what the doctors saw with their scopes.

An organism is devoured when it's eaten by another organism.

Doctors saw one organism eating another.

2. How can you tell that the disease was **lethal**?

_____

_____

3. Why must a disease be **diagnosed**?

_____

_____

4. What **plea** did Dr. Vaughan **intercept**?

_____

_____

5. Why do you think the disease was often passed at **rendezvous** points?

_____

_____

6. How can someone get sick when they have on a mask? Describe how the organism **seeped** into the masks.

_____

_____

© Harcourt

The 1918 Epidemic

by Susan Blackaby

illustrated by Craig Orback

In 1918, the health of the United States was in peril. An epidemic swept across the land. When it was over, many people had lost their lives.

The illness started at a fort in Kansas on a spring morning. A man reported to the doctor. He was feeling ill. It didn't seem that bad. But in a short time, a second man came in. He had the same problem. At lunch time, one hundred men were sick. In a week, five hundred men were sick. In all, forty-eight men passed away, while the rest got well. The illness seemed to vanish . . . for a while.

At the time, the United States was involved in a world-wide war across the Atlantic. **1**

Stop and Think

1 How can you tell that the illness is easy to catch?

I can tell that it's easy to catch because _____

_____

_____

Men were drafted into the army and sent across the sea. Some of the men were from the fort in Kansas. When they set sail, the puzzling illness went with them. In no time, men on the ships and in battle came down with it. The illness passed from man to man. It gained strength. When at last it came back to the United States, the organism was lethal. ❷

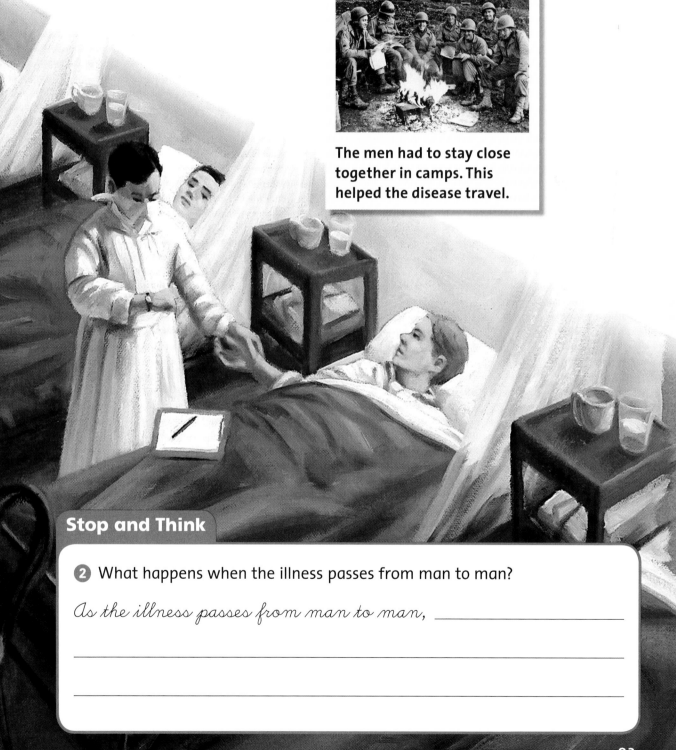

The men had to stay close together in camps. This helped the disease travel.

Stop and Think

❷ What happens when the illness passes from man to man?

As the illness passes from man to man, _____

_____

_____

The illness came back to the port in Boston. It was late summer. Doctors from a camp sent out a plea for help. A doctor named Victor Vaughan was the one to intercept the call. His orders were to get to the camp as fast as possible.

Victor arrived at the camp and was shocked at what he found. Hundreds were sick. The poor victims who did not have beds had to sleep on the floor. That next morning, sixty-three men had lost their lives. Doctors hadn't seen this illness in the past. They diagnosed it and called it the Spanish Flu. **3**

Stop and Think

3 What happens after the illness comes back to the United States?

After it comes back, the illness_____

_____

_____

© Harcourt

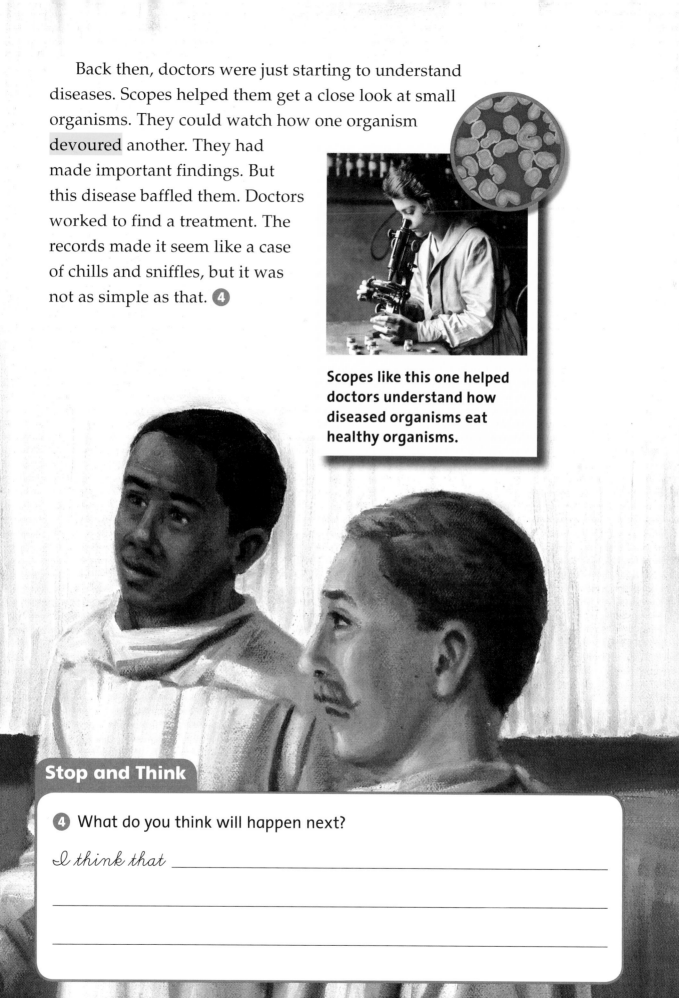

Back then, doctors were just starting to understand diseases. Scopes helped them get a close look at small organisms. They could watch how one organism devoured another. They had made important findings. But this disease baffled them. Doctors worked to find a treatment. The records made it seem like a case of chills and sniffles, but it was not as simple as that. **4**

Scopes like this one helped doctors understand how diseased organisms eat healthy organisms.

Stop and Think

4 What do you think will happen next?

I think that _____

_____

_____

In a normal case of the flu, you get some rest and feel better in a day or two. But this form of the flu was not a bit normal. How could such a small thing affect you so quickly? And how could it be stopped?

Just breathing put you at risk. One sneeze could infect a crowd. It seemed to follow the railroads, and at each railway rendezvous point, the disease was passed. It started with one case and infected hundreds. People strapped on masks to help keep the organisms at bay. But the organism seeped into the masks' small holes. **5**

A New York street cleaner wears a mask during the 1918 epidemic.

Stop and Think

5 Why does the disease seem to follow the railroads?

It seems to follow the railroads because _____

_____

_____

From the northeast, the disease went west. Some mayors were ignorant of how bad it was. They didn't want a major panic on their hands, so they didn't take steps to inform the public. By then, it was too late.

In a short time, doors on each street were decorated with black, white, or gray cloth. The cloth showed that a resident had died. Black and gray were for adults; white was for children. Shops and factories closed. Kids stayed home from class. In just one month, the disease claimed 12,000 lives. ❻

Crowds of people gather in the streets of New York City to celebrate the end of the war in 1918.

Stop and Think

❻ Why do the shops and factories close?

The shops and factories close because _____

_____

_____

From the beginning to the end of October, the disease killed 195,000 in the United States alone. It was like getting stuck in a storm. And like a storm, it passed. The organism killed all who could not stand up to it. Those who survived were now immune to the disease.

By May 1, the epidemic was over. Doctors were left with a new need to find out all they could from these small but strong organisms.

Over the years, doctors have discovered cures for many such diseases. They hope their hard work will ensure that an epidemic like the one in 1918 will never happen again. **7**

Today, doctors immunize people to protect them from the flu and other diseases.

Stop and Think

7 How is the epidemic like a storm?

It is like a storm because _____

_____

_____

88

Think Critically

1. What happened in the United States in 1918? Fill in the Main Idea box with your answer. MAIN IDEA AND DETAILS

Detail	**Detail**	**Detail**
The disease spread fast.	Doctors tried to treat it.	Many people died.

Main Idea

2. What happened after the epidemic was over? CAUSE AND EFFECT

After the epidemic was over, _____

_____

_____

3. Why is it important to remember these events? AUTHOR'S PURPOSE

It's important to remember these events because

_____

_____

altitude

equipped

extent

hampered

overshadowed

rely

reserve

Vocabulary

Build Robust Vocabulary

Write the Vocabulary Word that completes each sentence in the newspaper articles. The first one has been done for you.

© Harcourt

DAILY NEWS   SECTION C

DAILY N

Event Held for Volunteers

by Mark Mead

Monday, June 26

An event is being held to show respect for our volunteer fire department. The entire town is invited to come to the park on Main Street this weekend. There will be a lot of fun and games for everyone to enjoy.

Small towns like ours **(1)** _____ rely _____ on volunteers at the fire department. They help save homes, stores, and barns. They save lives, too.

Volunteers are trained and

(2) _____

with gear. In our town, they often battle high

(3) _____

fires in the upper, remote hills. These volunteers put their lives on the line, but do not get paid.

Volunteer Fire Department Saves Home

by Mark Mead

Monday, July 3

Over the weekend, the volunteer fire department responded to a fire at the Smith home. The fire started in the hay by the barn. Strong winds fed the flames and **(4)** _____ the fire team's efforts. In the end, the team put the fire out before it got to the home.

The department said they had the equipment they needed. If not for that, the **(5)** _____ of the fire could have reached the home. Our small town does not have extra money in **(6)** _____ funds. Our volunteers are glad that other fire departments in big towns sent equipment to us.

We often hear more about big fire departments in the news. Small fire departments seem to be **(7)** _____ by the bigger ones. It's important that we do not forget how much we need our volunteer fire department.

THE VOLUNTEERS

by Frank Coffin

The fire begins in the dark, inside a faded-red barn. Before long, the flames eat up the hay and then attack the barn's rotting boards. Hundreds of sparks soar up and float away like little stars.

Who will come to put out the flames? Many small towns don't have full-time firefighters. They rely on volunteers. These people work at other jobs, but they agree to put out fires at any time. They don't get paid for risking their lives to battle fires. **1**

Stop and Think

1 What facts do you learn about volunteer firefighters?

I learn that volunteer firefighters _____

_____

_____

© Harcourt

Who are these volunteers? Some are teachers. Some work in stores. Others are carpenters or farmers. Whatever jobs they have, they drop everything when they hear the fire alarm. They rush to save a home, a barn, or a store, and the victims who could be trapped inside. Without them, many lives and homes would be lost. ②

Stop and Think

② Do you think that it would be difficult to be a volunteer firefighter? Explain.

I think that _____

_____

_____

volunteer firefighter

Of course, you hear more about big fire departments, so volunteer fire departments may seem overshadowed by them. In fact, two out of three fire departments in the United States are made up of volunteers rather than paid workers. And there are three times more volunteers who battle fires than there are paid workers.

For the most part, volunteer fire departments are the same as other fire departments. People who volunteer are trained, equipped, and willing to put their lives on the line for others. ③

Stop and Think

③ How are volunteer firefighters like paid firefighters?

Both are _____

_____

_____

Most towns that form volunteer fire departments are in remote areas, such as the mountains. The high altitude in the mountains raises the risk of forest fires. It could take a long time for faraway fire trucks to arrive.

These small communities set up a Fire Board to plan and run the volunteer fire department. The citizens pick volunteers for the Fire Board.

First, the Board creates a complete plan for the new department. The Board says what areas the fire department will protect, how they'll get and store equipment, and how many volunteers they'll need. **4**

volunteer firefighter

Stop and Think

4 How does a Fire Board plan a fire department?

A Fire Board _____

_____

_____

The biggest chore in forming a volunteer fire department is planning how to pay for it. Big cities may have reserve funds from taxes that small towns don't. Getting trucks and other equipment and training volunteers takes time, money, and planning.

Volunteer fire departments sometimes seek grants to help pay for what they need. Or they ask bigger fire departments to send them extra equipment. It may take a long time before a new department can start working. **5**

volunteer firefighter

Stop and Think

5 What does a community need to form a volunteer fire department?

A community needs _____

_____

_____

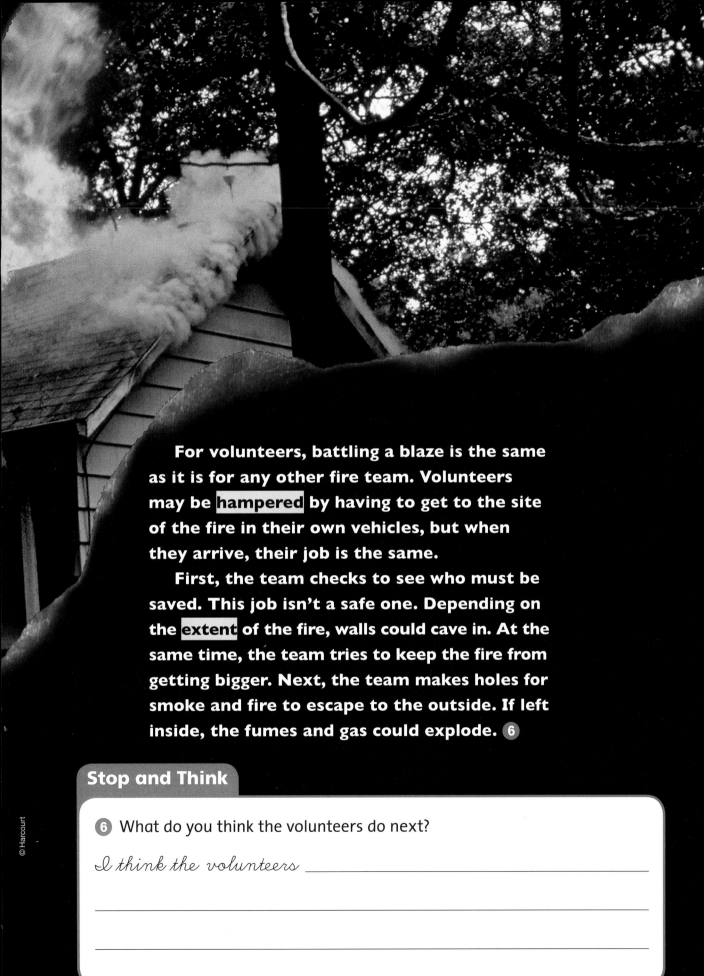

For volunteers, battling a blaze is the same as it is for any other fire team. Volunteers may be hampered by having to get to the site of the fire in their own vehicles, but when they arrive, their job is the same.

First, the team checks to see who must be saved. This job isn't a safe one. Depending on the extent of the fire, walls could cave in. At the same time, the team tries to keep the fire from getting bigger. Next, the team makes holes for smoke and fire to escape to the outside. If left inside, the fumes and gas could explode. **6**

Stop and Think

6 What do you think the volunteers do next?

I think the volunteers _____

_____

_____

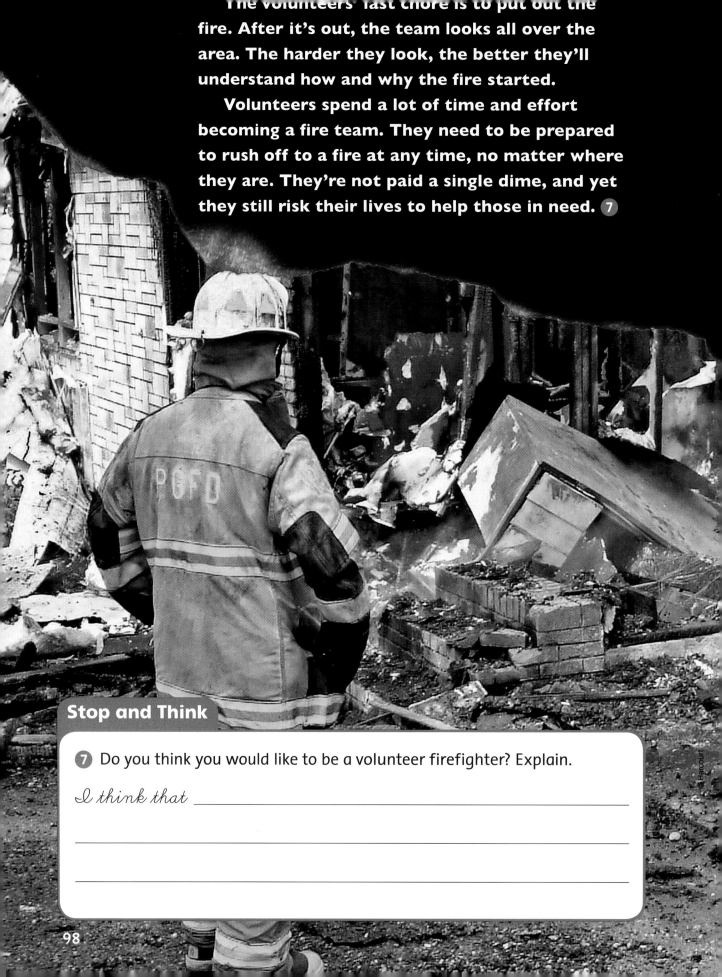

The volunteers' last chore is to put out the fire. After it's out, the team looks all over the area. The harder they look, the better they'll understand how and why the fire started.

Volunteers spend a lot of time and effort becoming a fire team. They need to be prepared to rush off to a fire at any time, no matter where they are. They're not paid a single dime, and yet they still risk their lives to help those in need. **7**

Stop and Think

7 Do you think you would like to be a volunteer firefighter? Explain.

I think that _____

_____

_____

Think Critically

1. What do you learn about volunteer fire departments? Fill in the Main Idea box with your answer. **MAIN IDEA AND DETAILS**

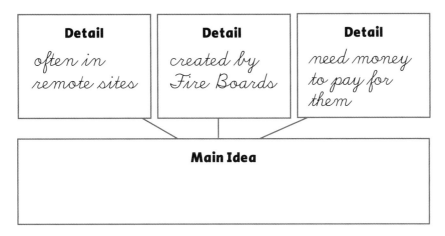

Detail	Detail	Detail
often in remote sites	created by Fire Boards	need money to pay for them

Main Idea

2. What might happen in a community that doesn't have enough funds? **CAUSE AND EFFECT**

    The community might _____

    _____

    _____

3. How do you think the author feels about volunteer firefighters? **AUTHOR'S PURPOSE**

    I think the author feels _____

    _____

    _____

Vocabulary

Build Robust Vocabulary

Write the Vocabulary Word that best completes each sentence. The first one has been done for you.

1. A garter snake is missing from class. Mr. Burnside could

   _____ **confront** _____ the kids about this.

   concede   unearth   confront

2. But Mr. Burnside will _____ that

   vie   concede   diagnose

   he may not have put the screen back on the snake's tank.

3. Carla feels silly, but she _____

   confidentially   ordinarily   sheepishly

   takes a peek to see if the snake is under her desk.

4. Marcus states that he didn't do it. "I know that I'm not the

   _____," he says.

   culprit   scandal   alibi

5. Marcus was absent yesterday. He has the perfect

   _____.

   altitude   alibi   scandal

© Harcourt

6. Mr. Burnside says, "There's no

_____ to think that

alibi   justification   culprit

one of you is to blame."

7. Marcus doesn't want to start a panic. "Let's keep

this development _____

sheepish   conceded   confidential

until we first search the lab."

8. Arthur says, "I can see it all now. Escaped snake terrorizes

staff and kids. What a _____ that

scandal   justification   culprit

would be!"

9. Derwin says, "Escaped snake is

_____ in trash bin!

vying   reserved   unearthed

Janitor faints from shock!"

10. The kids are _____ to come up

vying   conceding   confronting

with the best comical plot that involves the escaped snake.

Write the answers to these questions. Use complete sentences.

11. What are you doing if you confront someone?

_____

_____

12. How can an alibi help Marcus?

_____

_____

The Case of the Missing Garter Snake

by Barbara Adams

illustrated by Kristin Sorra

Characters

Mr. Burnside	Arthur
Carla	Marcus
Derwin	Ann
Chorus	

Narrator: The kids in Mr. Burnside's class are researching reptiles. Yesterday they observed a garter snake firsthand. This morning when they got to the lab, they could tell that Mr. Burnside was upset. Will he confront them with what he has discovered?

Mr. Burnside: When I got to the lab this morning, I checked the tank to see if the garter snake had eaten the earthworms yet. To my surprise, I discovered that the snake was missing. Someone must have forgotten to put the screen back on the tank! ❶

Stop and Think

❶ Why is Mr. Burnside upset?

Mr. Burnside is upset because _____

_____

_____

Chorus: EEEEEK! An escaped snake!

Carla: It's just a garter snake. It's not going to hurt anyone.

Ann: But there's no telling where it is. It could be under your desk!

Narrator: Carla sheepishly takes a peek to see if the snake is there. She's glad that it isn't.

Mr. Burnside: Ann, would you please get down off your desk before you fall and hurt yourself? **2**

Stop and Think

2 How do you think Ann feels about snakes? How do you know?

I think Ann feels _____

_____

_____

Marcus: Well, Mr. Burnside, I know that I'm not the culprit. I have the perfect alibi. I was absent yesterday!

Derwin: Well, I was here yesterday, but it wasn't my turn to feed the snake.

Mr. Burnside: There's no justification to think that one of you is to blame. In fact, I concede that I could be the one who forgot to put the screen back on the tank.

Marcus: Umm, let's keep this development confidential until we first search the lab. If it gets out that our snake is roaming around free, it could start a panic.

Chorus: We don't want that to happen! ❸

Stop and Think

❸ Do you think Mr. Burnside is a fair teacher? Why do you think so?

Mr. Burnside _____

_____

_____

Arthur: I can see it all now. Escaped snake terrorizes staff and kids. What a scandal that would be!

Derwin: Yup! Garter snake escapes from lab on Thursday morning and is unearthed in trash bin days later! Janitor faints from shock!

Carla: All classes are dismissed for the day as volunteers search for missing snake!

Narrator: While the kids are vying to come up with comical plots, Mr. Burnside interrupts.

Mr. Burnside: Kids, kids, kids! We've got to find that snake now. ④

Stop and Think

④ How do the kids view the problem of the escaped snake? How can you tell?

The kids view the problem as _____

_____

_____

Arthur: I've got it! Let's pair up and then each search a different part of the lab.

Mr. Burnside: That's a terrific plan. You and Marcus search the closet. Ann and Carla, you two can look around the plants. Derwin and I will check out some of the other spots a snake could hide.

Ann: What do we do if or when we find the snake?

Mr. Burnside: There's no need for you to fret, Ann. I'll collect the snake *when* we find it and return it to the tank. **5**

Stop and Think

5 Does Mr. Burnside think they will find the snake? How can you tell?

Mr. Burnside thinks _____

_____

_____

Narrator: Mr. Burnside and the kids begin searching. After a short time, they meet back at Mr. Burnside's desk, without the snake. While Arthur is speaking, Ann happens to look over at a shelf where Mr. Burnside keeps some of his lab equipment and interrupts Arthur.

Ann: Excuse me, Arthur, but I think we missed some of the spots where a snake could hide. Look over there.

Narrator: Mr. Burnside and the rest of the kids turn to look at the shelf. **6**

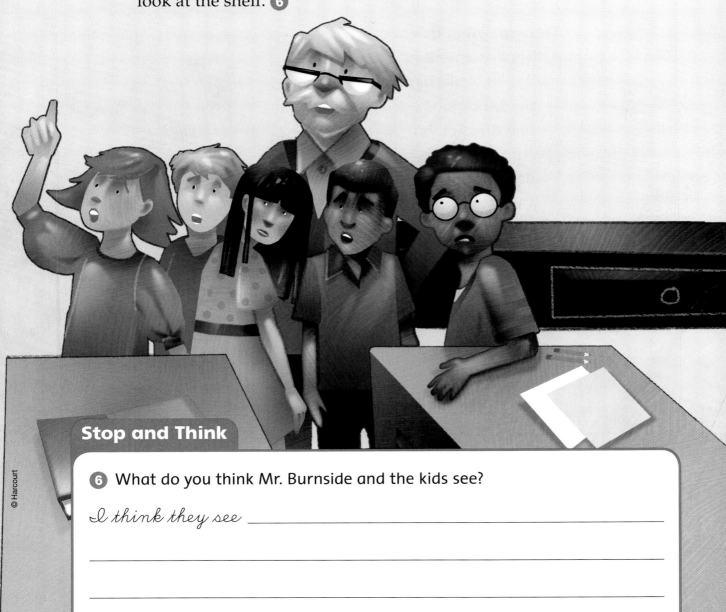

Stop and Think

6 What do you think Mr. Burnside and the kids see?

I think they see _____

_____

_____

Carla: It's the snake on the top shelf! Good spotting, Ann!

Chorus: Yes, we're so glad!

Mr. Burnside: Well, kids, you solved the case of the missing garter snake. Let's all learn from my mistake. We don't want this to happen again.

Arthur: Marcus and I will get the stepladder for you, Mr. Burnside, so you can get the snake. Come on, Marcus.

Derwin: Well, this has been an interesting day. It could have turned out to be a real disaster, but Ann saved the day *and* our garter snake! **7**

Stop and Think

7 What does Mr. Burnside want the kids to learn from this?

Mr. Burnside wants them to learn _____

_____

_____

Think Critically

1. **What caused the snake to escape?** CAUSE AND EFFECT

   The snake escaped because _____

   _____

   _____

   _____

2. **What might have happened if the kids hadn't found the snake in the lab?** PLOT

   If the snake hadn't been found, then _____

   _____

   _____

   _____

3. **Do you think this story could really happen? Why do you think so?** AUTHOR'S CRAFT

   I think that _____

   _____

   _____

   _____

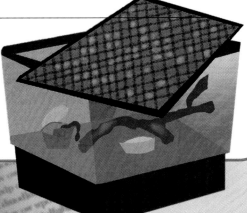

109

abundant
bearable
illuminates
phenomenon
refuge
thrive

Vocabulary

Build Robust Vocabulary

Write the Vocabulary Word that completes each sentence in the selection. The first one has been done for you.

The Ice Continent

Antarctica is a continent with an **(1)** _____**abundant**_____ supply of ice. There is plenty of it. The sun does not shine in the winter. It **(2)** _____ the continent for only part of the year. The long days of sunshine make the chilly summer more **(3)** _____. In winter, it is harder to stand the cold. Dark days and freezing cold make it hard to survive.

Antarctica is filled with animals that seem to **(4)** _____ in the bitter cold. How can they live there? Explorers travel to Antarctica to study these animals. On any trip, explorers may find a new kind of animal or a new **(5)** _____ in nature. However, people are not equipped to survive for long stretches of time in Antarctica. They must find **(6)** _____ from the cold by making shelters and staying warm.

In 1914, some sailors discovered that it would take all their skills to survive a trip to the ice continent. You will read about their adventure in "Stranded on the Ice."

STRANDED ON THE ICE

by David Neufeld

In the fall of 1914, the ship *Endurance* set sail on what would be a heroic trip to Antarctica. On board were two men who approached the journey with the same adventurous spirit, but in very different ways. Ernest Shackleton planned to pilot the ship. Frank Hurley planned to take pictures along the way. Both men had been to Antarctica before.

A skilled sea captain, Shackleton asked Hurley to record the historic trip. Hurley was an artist who was respected for his images of barren landscapes. Each man would be tested in the months to come. The land of lethal cold wasn't **bearable** to those who had been there before. ❶

Stop and Think

❶ What do you want to know about this trip?

I want to know _____

_____

_____

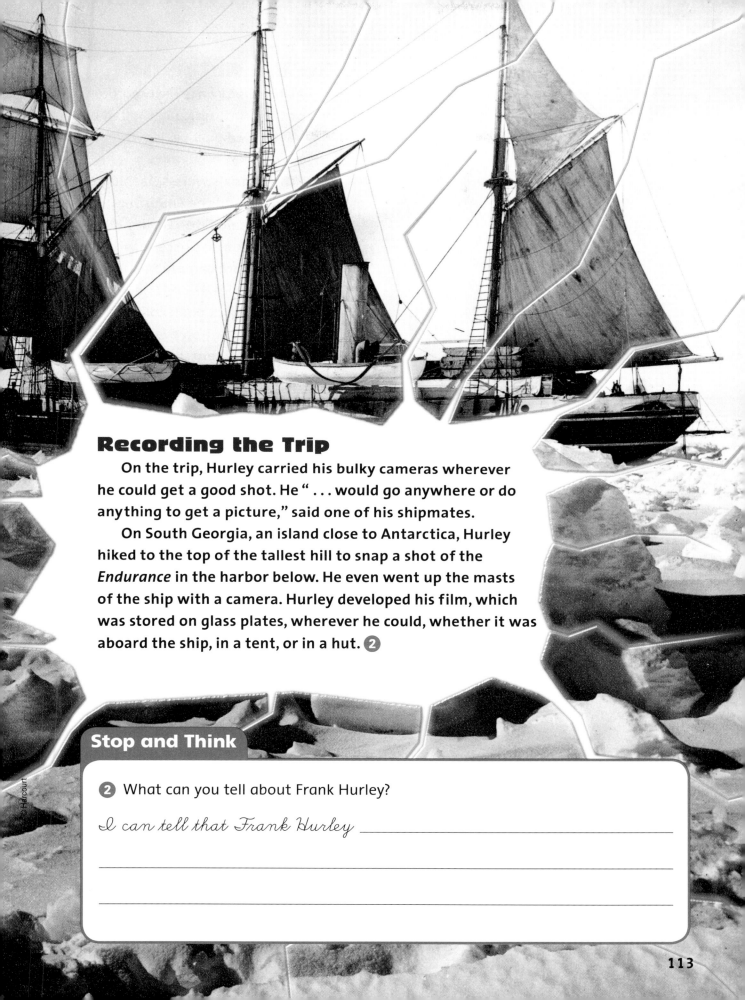

Recording the Trip

On the trip, Hurley carried his bulky cameras wherever he could get a good shot. He " . . . would go anywhere or do anything to get a picture," said one of his shipmates.

On South Georgia, an island close to Antarctica, Hurley hiked to the top of the tallest hill to snap a shot of the *Endurance* in the harbor below. He even went up the masts of the ship with a camera. Hurley developed his film, which was stored on glass plates, wherever he could, whether it was aboard the ship, in a tent, or in a hut. **2**

Stop and Think

2 What can you tell about Frank Hurley?

I can tell that Frank Hurley _____

_____

_____

© Harcourt

To the Antarctic!

As the *Endurance* entered the seas off of Antarctica in the fall of 1914, it sailed past seals swimming offshore.

"The animals were splashing and blowing around the *Endurance*," Shackleton said later. Hurley made a film of this fantastic scene with his moving-picture camera.

In Antarctica, there's no warm air. If it's not just plain cold, it's freezing cold. But on every trip to the chilly continent, explorers might possibly find some new animal or new **phenomenon**. Amazingly, Antarctica has many animals. They seem to **thrive** in the bitter cold. **3**

Hurley recorded penguins and other animals.

Stop and Think

3 Why do you think the author describes Antarctica?

I think he describes Antarctica because _____

_____

_____

Hurley captured the ship's final moments on film.

Trapped!

Pack ice covers miles of sea water in Antarctica. Pack ice is what sea water around land turns into when it freezes. In 1914, it broke up late, let the *Endurance* in closer to land, and then froze solid again. The ship was trapped in the ice.

The men tried to cut the ice from around the ship. Some days the ship moved yards forward, but the freezing ice continued to push against it. As strong as this ship was constructed, it couldn't handle the pressure from the ice. The ice crushed the ship like a tin can. The men stayed on board as long as they could. Finally, it became too risky for them to remain. They abandoned the ship just before it broke apart. **4**

Stop and Think

4 What do you think the men will do next?

I think the men will _____

_____

_____

Surviving on the Ice

The men found refuge on the ice, using tents as shelters. Suspended on the ice, the broken ship protected them from the winds. Hurley went back to the ship and dove into the freezing water to save some of his glass plates. Later, he and Shackleton looked them over and chose 120 to save. The rest they broke.

Shackleton led his men across the ice, trying to find more solid land. They dragged the lifeboats with them, and Hurley dragged his treasured plates. The ice was like a frozen puzzle, shifting and cracking as they walked over it.

Months later, Shackleton and his men reached Elephant Island, where they would spend a year of their lives. **5**

The men survived on the ice for months before searching for land.

Stop and Think

5 How is the ice like a frozen puzzle?

The ice is like a frozen puzzle because _____

_____

_____

The men used lifeboats and tents as shelters.

An Attempt at Rescue

On April 24, 1916, Shackleton and two men set sail in a tiny repaired life boat, trying to reach South Georgia Island. Twenty-two men were left behind to wait for a later rescue.

During the stormy trip, the men had to chip ice from the deck of the lifeboat so it wouldn't sink. They sailed in waves five stories tall. When they reached South Georgia Island, hurricane winds wouldn't let them sail around to the harbor where help might be found. They almost crashed into the rocks, but at the last minute they passed by them. The next morning, they landed on the far side in a bay. Still, miles of hard hiking separated them from help. **6**

Stop and Think

6 How do you think the men who were left behind felt?

I think the men felt _____

_____

_____

117

A Daring Rescue!

Months passed from the day Shackleton and the two men had sailed off for help. The men left behind began to lose hope in rescue. While they waited, the abundant sunlight increased their risk of snow blindness. In Antarctica, the sun illuminates the stark whiteness of the snow, blinding those who look at it for too long.

Then on August 30, 1916, out of the mist came a small ship. Shackleton had made it to safety—and had returned to rescue his men! While they left the *Endurance* behind, the explorers had gained something even more important: real endurance. Not a single person died, and Frank Hurley captured it all on film. **7**

Stop and Think

7 How do you feel about this selection's ending?

I feel _____

_____

_____

Think Critically

1. What did you learn about the trip? Fill in the third column of the K-W-L chart with your answers. **MAIN IDEA AND DETAILS**

K What I Know	W What I Want to Know	L What I Learned

2. What did you learn about Ernest Shackleton? **CHARACTERS' TRAITS**

   I learned that Ernest Shackleton _____

   _____

   _____

3. How did the men gain endurance? **CAUSE AND EFFECT**

   They gained endurance by _____

   _____

   _____

| blurted |
| ideal |
| pelting |
| perched |
| slunk |
| stranded |
| wedged |

Vocabulary

Build Robust Vocabulary

Write the Vocabulary Word that completes each sentence. The first one has been done for you.

"This is an **(1)** _____ideal_____ time for a hike into Stone Mount State Park," said Luis. It was the best day for a hike because it was so perfect outside. Robert agreed to take a quick hike up the mountain with his new pals Luis and Kiley.

After they had hiked for about an hour, Robert climbed up a tree. He **(2)** _____ on a branch and looked at the forest around him. Then an odd sound startled him. He scrambled down from the tree.

The sound was coming from somewhere near the ground. "Look!" Kiley **(3)** _____ out.

There was a baby owl **(4)** _____ on the
ground. It couldn't fly because its wing was broken. "What
do we do?" Robert asked.

Just then, fat raindrops began **(5)** _____ the
hikers like rocks. Rain began gathering in a puddle around
the little owl. Robert felt that the owl would drown if they
left it there.

Robert carefully wrapped his jacket around the owl. He
slowly lifted up the bundle and **(6)** _____ it
under his arm, making sure he didn't hurt the owl.

When Robert got home later that day, he was an
hour late and soaking wet. He **(7)** _____
into the house, hoping his mom wouldn't see him.

Write the Vocabulary Word that best completes the synonym web.

8.

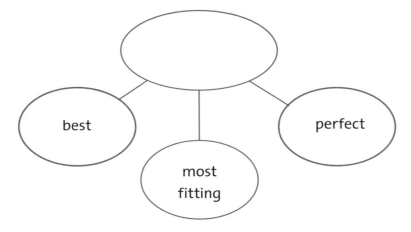

- best
- perfect
- most fitting

The Long Hike

by Wiley Gaby

illustrated by Pedro Rodriguez

"Come on, Robert, let's go!" called Luis as he slung his backpack on his back. "It's perfect out, and this is an ideal time for a hike into Stone Mount State Park."

I had just moved from a big city to Stone Mount, a small town nestled in the mountains. Stone Mount was a lot different from my old home. There, I had hiked to the subway lots of times, but never up a mountain!

My new pals, Luis and Kiley, wanted to show me Stone Mount State Park after class, so I agreed to take a quick hike up the mountain with them. ❶

Stop and Think

❶ What details do you learn about the narrator? Underline them in the story.

I learn that _____

_____

_____

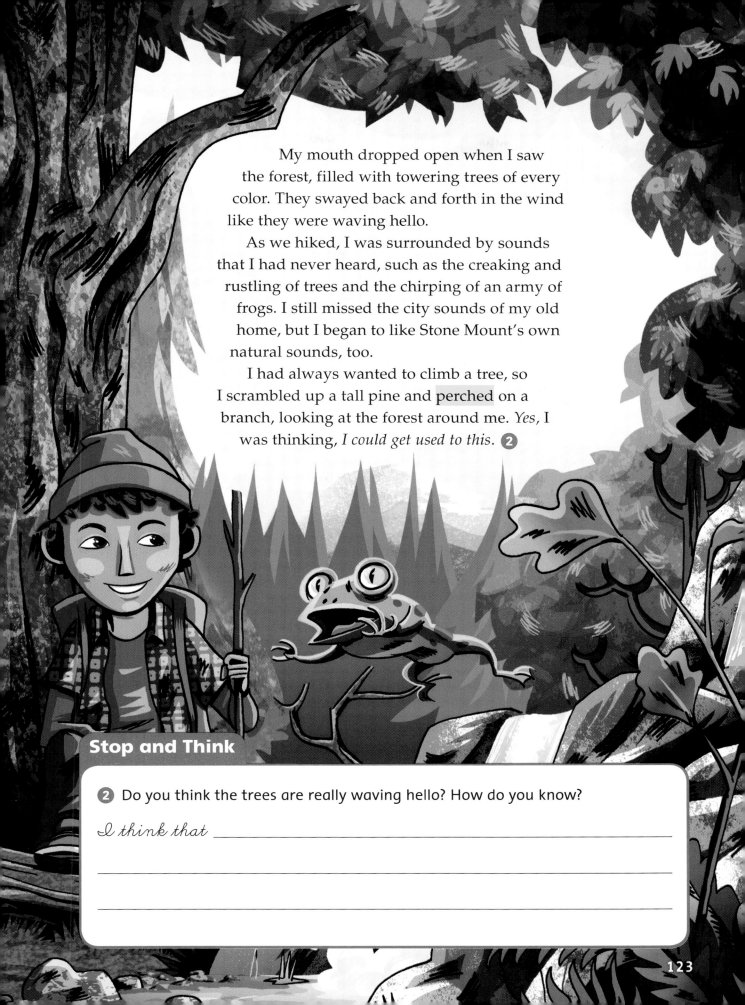

My mouth dropped open when I saw the forest, filled with towering trees of every color. They swayed back and forth in the wind like they were waving hello.

As we hiked, I was surrounded by sounds that I had never heard, such as the creaking and rustling of trees and the chirping of an army of frogs. I still missed the city sounds of my old home, but I began to like Stone Mount's own natural sounds, too.

I had always wanted to climb a tree, so I scrambled up a tall pine and perched on a branch, looking at the forest around me. *Yes*, I was thinking, *I could get used to this.* ❷

Stop and Think

❷ Do you think the trees are really waving hello? How do you know?

I think that _____

_____

_____

123

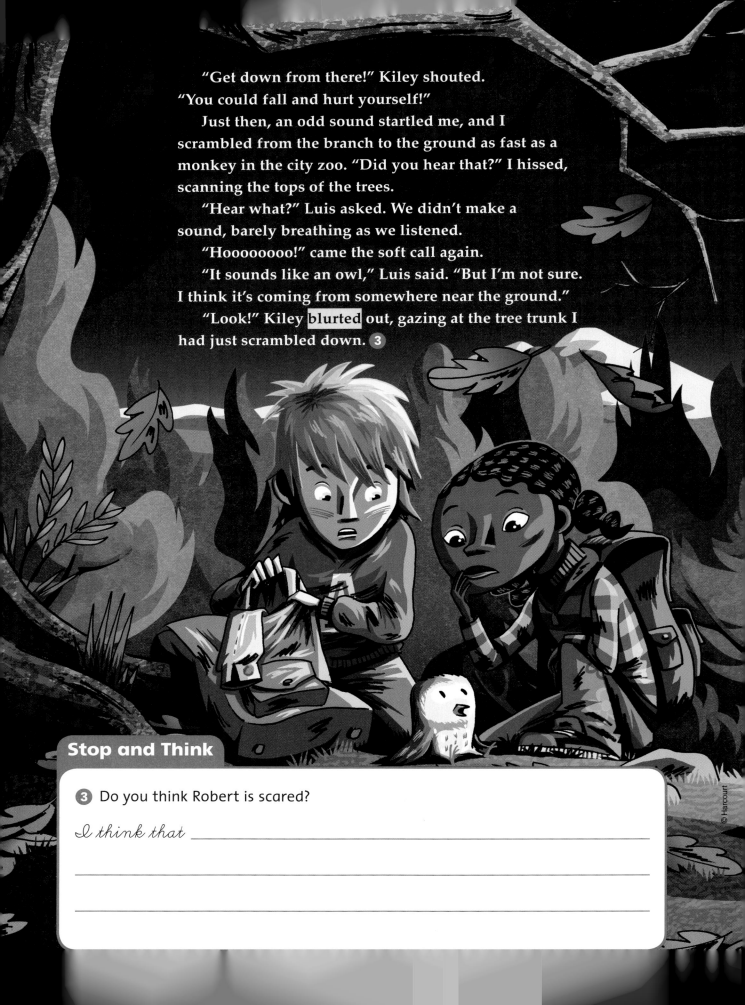

"Get down from there!" Kiley shouted. "You could fall and hurt yourself!"

Just then, an odd sound startled me, and I scrambled from the branch to the ground as fast as a monkey in the city zoo. "Did you hear that?" I hissed, scanning the tops of the trees.

"Hear what?" Luis asked. We didn't make a sound, barely breathing as we listened.

"Hoooooooo!" came the soft call again.

"It sounds like an owl," Luis said. "But I'm not sure. I think it's coming from somewhere near the ground."

"Look!" Kiley blurted out, gazing at the tree trunk I had just scrambled down. 3

Stop and Think

3 Do you think Robert is scared?

I think that _____

_____

_____

© Harcourt

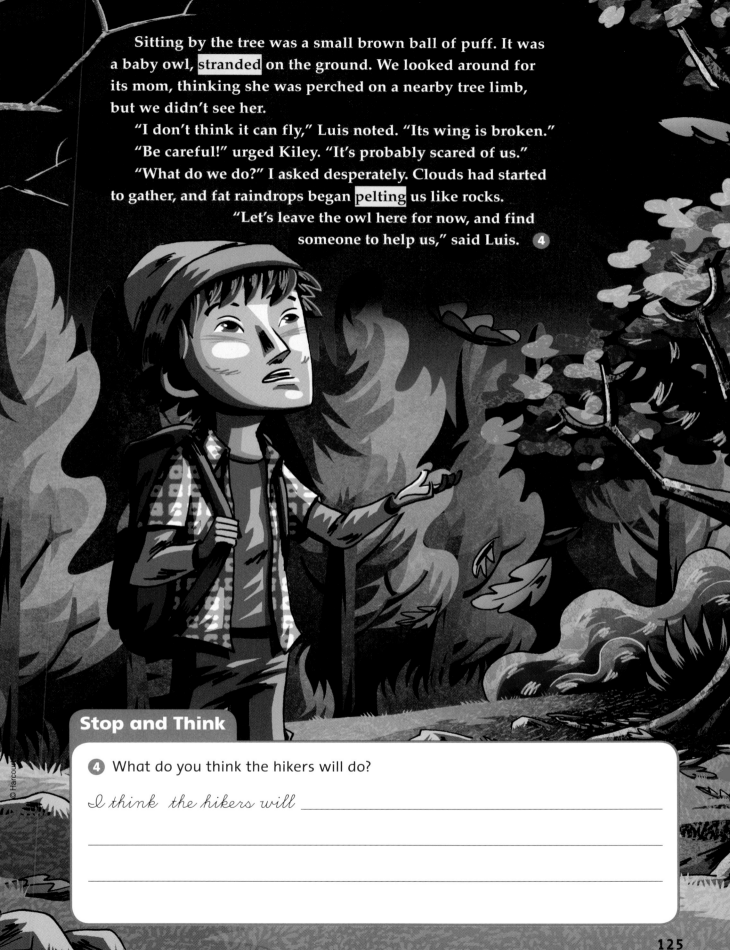

Sitting by the tree was a small brown ball of puff. It was a baby owl, stranded on the ground. We looked around for its mom, thinking she was perched on a nearby tree limb, but we didn't see her.

"I don't think it can fly," Luis noted. "Its wing is broken."

"Be careful!" urged Kiley. "It's probably scared of us."

"What do we do?" I asked desperately. Clouds had started to gather, and fat raindrops began pelting us like rocks.

"Let's leave the owl here for now, and find someone to help us," said Luis. ④

Stop and Think

④ What do you think the hikers will do?

I think the hikers will _____

_____

_____

"No!" I blurted out, adding, "Let's take it *with* us to find someone who can help."

I had a feeling that the owl would drown if we left it there, so I carefully wrapped my jacket around the owl. I slowly lifted up the bundle and wedged it under my arm, making sure I didn't squeeze it too much.

We ran back to school just in time to catch Miss Garza, who was just leaving.

"My sister will know just what to do for this little bird," she assured us. "She's a vet." **5**

Stop and Think

5 What can you tell about Robert?

I can tell that _____

_____

_____

When I finally made it home, I slunk into the house, hoping my mom wouldn't see me. But I had no such luck.

"Where have you been, Robert? I expected you home an hour ago!"

"But, Mom," I said, "I'm late for a good reason." I tried to explain why the hike had taken so long.

"We'll talk about it later!" she interrupted. "Your clothes are a mess, and is that a feather? Just go take a shower." **6**

Stop and Think

6 Why are Robert's clothes messy?

Robert's clothes are messy because _____

_____

_____

The next day, while Dad watched the news, I happened to see a little brown ball of fluff flash onto the screen.

"That's the owl I found!" I blurted out, gazing at a smiling vet in a white coat holding the baby owl. My mom walked into the den to see what all the fuss was about.

"Some students from Stone Mount found this baby owl during yesterday's storm and made sure it got the help it needed," the vet was saying.

"So that's what you were doing yesterday!" Mom exclaimed. "I had wondered about all of those feathers."

"So . . . are you still mad at me?" I asked with a grin. **7**

Stop and Think

7 Do you think Robert's parents are still mad at him? Explain.

I think that Robert's parents _____

_____

_____

Think Critically

1. How is Robert's new home different from his old home?
COMPARE AND CONTRAST

Robert's new home is _____

_____

_____

2. What problem does Robert encounter when he returns home?
How is it resolved? Fill in the story map with your answers. PLOT

Conflict

Resolution

3. How do you think the author feels about helping animals?
Explain your answer. AUTHOR'S PURPOSE

I think the author feels that helping animals _____

_____

_____

Vocabulary

disoriented

haphazardly

imperative

optimistic

premonition

receded

remorse

Build Robust Vocabulary

Write the Vocabulary Word that completes each sentence. The first one has been done for you.

Raj had to stay at home with Nani while his parents were out of town. His parents had said it was

(1) _____imperative_____ for him to take care of Nani while they were away.

Raj liked to hear Nani tell stories of the old days and of events that happened long ago.

Nani told Raj about one time when a big rain came and filled the streets with water. The high waters had made it hard for Nani to know where she was. Like her, other people were

(2) _____ too. But in the end, the waters

(3) _____, and life got back to normal.

©Harcourt

One day, while his parents were still out of town, Raj was out playing with his pet birds. The birds started flying about randomly. They went on flying **(4)** _____ back and forth. To Raj, it seemed that their strange behavior was a **(5)** _____. He felt that something bad was about to happen.

Raj remembered that he had left Nani at home alone. He felt **(6)** _____ about that. He hoped that she was okay. He hurried back to check on her.

When Raj got home, he told Nani about the birds. She also felt that something bad was about to happen. She didn't seem very **(7)** _____.

Write the answers to these questions. Use complete sentences.

8. What does it mean if a task is imperative?

_____

_____

9. What can make a person feel remorse?

_____

_____

Run for the Hills!

by Karin Vonesh

illustrated by Danuta Wojciechowska

I watched the bright colors of my two pet birds flying across the darkening skies, the sounds of their screeching filling the night. "Atul, Amal, stop fighting!" I called.

My mom and dad were off at a faraway town down the coast, selling their paintings and pottery. I had stayed behind to care for Nani. I'd promised my parents that I'd take good care of her while they traveled. I didn't mind, for this gave me more time to spend with Nani and my birds. **1**

Stop and Think

1 What do you learn about the characters and setting?

I learn that _____

_____

_____

© Harcourt

"Amal, Atul, come down!" I yelled, calling
for the birds to perch on my arm. But they wouldn't
listen and kept flying haphazardly back and forth.
   How odd! I wondered, gazing up at the birds.
They were usually so calm, but now they seemed so
disoriented that they were about to tie themselves up
in the vines. *What is it about tonight?* I asked myself,
looking around at the darkening hills. **2**

Stop and Think

2 Why do you think the birds are behaving so strangely?

I think the birds are behaving strangely because _____

_____

_____

The strange behavior of my birds worried me. I hurried back home, eager to tell Nani what I'd seen.

Right away, Nani could sense my fright. "What is it, Raj?" she asked me as I met her at the door. I told her about the birds fighting in the skies and how their odd behavior seemed to be a premonition that something was about to happen.

"Animals can tell us many things," she agreed with a wise nod. "Watch the birds again at first light, and tell me right away if they are still acting strangely." ③

Stop and Think

③ What do you learn about Nani?

I learn that Nani _____

_____

_____

I was awake for most of the night, worried about my birds. In the morning, I ran to check on them, but they weren't there—Amal and Atul had flown away! Even more distressed than before, I went to wake Nani.

"Raj, I believe the birds' behavior was indeed a premonition," Nani explained as she shuffled to the door. "Do you feel the wind that rises and dies?" she asked with a frown. "It tells me of something frightening. And the flight of animals makes me think it is a very high wave that will come and cover the town. It's imperative that you tell everyone to follow the animals and go to higher ground." **4**

Stop and Think

4 What do you think will happen next?

I think that _____

_____

_____

"I must warn the tourists, too!" I exclaimed, thinking of the tourists who came to see our sparkling white beaches. I ran down to the shoreline and reached the hotel just as sunlight started to glisten on the water.

"A high wave is coming, and it will engulf the town, so you must run for the hills!" I told the tourists.

"You can't be right!" one man said. "Today is an ideal day for swimming. No high wave will ruin it."

"Please!" I begged. "Don't be so optimistic. We must listen to the animals' warning!"

Finally, the tourists became alarmed and returned to the hotel to gather their belongings. **5**

Stop and Think

5 What problem does Raj have?

Raj's problem is _____

_____

_____

© Harcourt

Later, Nani and I struggled up the winding path, going higher and higher into the hills. "Raj, I must stop," gasped Nani. "I'm too old, and my legs are weak."

"If you can't walk, then I'll carry you." I put Nani's light frame over my back and carried her up into the hills, staggering back and forth on the steep slopes.

After a while, my legs felt like rubber and I didn't think I could go one more step. *Why did my parents think I could take care of Nani?* I wondered. *I'm just a kid, and a weak one, too.* I wished Nani could walk by herself, and I felt the burden of the promise I'd made to my parents. **6**

Stop and Think

6 How does Raj feel about his promise?

Raj feels _____

_____

_____

© Harcourt

Finally, we made it to the top, where everyone had gathered to watch the high wave cover the land. Some of the people were holding their most cherished belongings. I was holding mine—Nani. I felt remorse for my earlier resentment about caring for Nani. We'd made it, hadn't we? I had carried her up the steep slopes to safety . . . all by myself.

We stayed on the hill until it grew dark. We couldn't tell if the waters had receded or not. Suddenly, we heard a screeching and looked up to see the shadowy forms of my birds. The birds' leaving was a warning, but their return was a sign that the danger had passed. We were safe. 7

Stop and Think

7 What lesson does Raj learn from his experience?

Raj learns that _____

_____

_____

©Harcourt

Think Critically

1. How did the birds, Nani, and Raj all help to save people from the giant wave? Write the plot events in the story map. PLOT

Conflict
giant wave

Plot Events

1. *The birds*

2. *Nani*

3. *Raj*

Resolution
animals and people are saved

2. Why does the author include Raj's thoughts in the story?
AUTHOR'S PURPOSE

The author includes Raj's thoughts because _____

_____

_____

3. How does Raj feel now that he has helped save Nani and the rest of the people? CHARACTER

Raj feels _____

_____

_____

acquaintance

cocky

gingerly

rank

retrieve

stymied

terminal

winced

Vocabulary

Build Robust Vocabulary

Write the Vocabulary Word that completes each sentence in the diary. The first one has been done for you.

Monday

There is nothing to do, and I am suffering from a

(1) _____ **terminal** _____ case of boredom! So far, our trip

has been rained out. It has rained all week!

When Ace asked me to play a hand of rummy again, I just

(2) _____ winced _____. We have played a hundred hands,

and he has won every time. I might not mind so much, but he gets so

(3) _____ cocky _____ when he wins. Yesterday, he said,

"Just call me the *Rummy Champ of the World*."

I teased him in return by saying, "Pleased to make your

(4) _____ acquantance _____. I do hope we can get to know

each other better."

Tuesday

 This morning we **(5)** _gingerly_ walked a short distance up the soggy trail. It was too slippery to go far. Ace's feet got soaked. His socks will smell **(6)** _rank_ later on if he doesn't dry them out!

 The sun is supposed to be out tomorrow. I went out to **(7)** _retrieve_ my backpack from Dad's car, just in case Ace decides to go hiking with me. I just hope I can keep up with him. He's not exactly thrilled about his little sister going with him. He says he'll be **(8)** _stymied_ and won't make it up the mountain if he has to drag me along.

Hiking with Ace

by Susan Blackaby

illustrated by Doug Bowles

"Wait, wait for me!" Nancy raced up the steep slope. Ace was by now far in front of her and had not even noticed when she lingered behind. Nancy had stopped to sketch a Pacific-slope Flycatcher that perched in a cedar tree. The bird had seemed to be sitting still just for her.

Ace hadn't been excited about taking his little sister on this outing in the first place, so Nancy was doing her best not to bug him.

Ace had laced up his hiking boots the instant the sun came up, and Nancy had begged to go with him. **1**

Stop and Think

1 What can you tell about the setting?

I can tell that _its on a mountian in a forest_

"No way," Ace had said, sounding cocky. "I want to travel light, which means no Nancy."

"I can't go on my own," she had pleaded. "Please let me go with you. You won't even know I'm there."

When she had convinced Ace to take her along, Nancy had gotten ready in a hurry. She had quickly stuffed her gear in her backpack before racing out the door.

Now, Nancy had to take twice as many steps to keep up with Ace's long strides, and her backpack bounced and bumped with every step. ❷

Stop and Think

❷ Why can't Nancy go hiking by herself?

Nancy can't go by herself because <u>just in case she gets hert or lost.</u>

"You're a terminal pack rat," teased Ace. "When I consider why you want to lug that backpack, I'm stymied. We have the entire mountain. What more do we need?"

But Nancy was glad to have her colored pencils and her sketch pad, and she knew Ace wouldn't pass up a snack.

The path led to a clearing. The top of the peak was in sight, but where was Ace? Nancy didn't think Ace would continue to the top without her.

She set down her backpack and circled around a little ways off the path. Ace was nowhere in sight. **3**

Stop and Think

3 How do you think Nancy feels?

I think Nancy feels <u>alone and scared</u>

Nancy decided to keep going up. She went to retrieve her backpack, and that's when she heard Ace call her name. The odd tone of his cry gave her a bad feeling.

Nancy found Ace down a slope, clutching his leg. His face showed that he was in pain.

"Pleased to make your acquaintance," he said, gritting his teeth. "Glad you decided to show up, since I've been calling you for around a century."

"What happened?" asked Nancy as she gingerly eased herself down the slope to reach him. **4**

Stop and Think

4 What do you think happened to Ace?

I think that Ace _fell and got hert or just resting_

© Harcourt

145

"I tripped over a log and twisted my leg," said Ace.

"Can you stand up?" asked Nancy as she clasped her arm around Ace's waist. "Hobble over to that tree," she instructed.

Ace sat down and leaned on the tree trunk. Nancy opened her backpack and offered Ace a bottle of water. Then she got out an instant cold pack, crushing it first to get it colder. Ace winced when she put the cold pack on his leg.

"Wow, Nancy," he said. "What else did you bring?"

"Everything but the kitchen sink, remember?" she replied with a grin. "Here, have a power bar." ⑤

Stop and Think

⑤ What does Ace discover about Nancy?

Ace discovers that Nancy ___was PerPared___

146

Nancy made certain that Ace was safe and then dashed back up to the clearing. She used rocks to make a big X and an arrow signaling toward their place underneath the tree. She filled the water flask at the creek before sliding back down the slope.

Then Nancy fished two plastic rain ponchos out of her backpack. They were plain, but bright yellow.

"My ponchos will help keep us warm," she said. "They'll be a cinch for Officer Garcia to spot, too."

"Is he also stuffed into your backpack?" joked Ace with a grin. **6**

Stop and Think

6 What do you think will happen next?

I think that _There gonna get rescue_

_____

_____

Nancy couldn't help giggling. "No, silly, but I did leave a note telling where we would be on the off chance that we got lost."

"I'm impressed, Nancy," said Ace, flashing a smile. "I'm never going anyplace without you ever again. But bring better power bars because this thing smells rank."

Nancy laughed, and the two talked about their next hiking trip as they waited for rescue. A while later, they heard the whirring sounds of a helicopter. Someone had seen Nancy's signal, and help was on the way.

"Do you happen to have some humble pie in your pack?" asked Ace, grinning. "I'm going to need it." **7**

Stop and Think

7 Why does Ace say he'll need some humble pie?

Ace says this because _____

_____

_____

© Harcourt

Think Critically

1. How does Nancy help to resolve the conflict in the story?
Fill in the resolution in the story map. PLOT

Conflict
Ace thinks Nancy will be a burden on the hike.

Resolution

2. What does the author teach you about judging others?
AUTHOR'S PURPOSE

   The author teaches me that _____

   _____

   _____

3. How does Ace feel at the beginning of the hike? How does he
feel at the end? COMPARE AND CONTRAST

   At the beginning, Ace feels _____

   _____

   At the end, Ace feels _____

   _____

© Harcourt

Vocabulary

Build Robust Vocabulary

Write the Vocabulary Word that best completes each sentence. The first one has been done for you.

1. Ages ago, many families gathered around a

_____**communal**_____ fire to hear stories.

prudent   dissatisfied   communal

2. Hearing a good story made them happy. It filled them with

_____ .

demands   bliss   remorse

3. One story tells about a time when there were no

sea tides to move the waters. The waters were

_____ .

dissatisfied   stationary   apparent

4. The Ancestors were _____ with

apparent   entwined   dissatisfied

this because they could not gather clams and crabs.

5. Then the Mighty Spirit sent Raven to the end of the

earth on an _____

arduous   apparent   entwined

task. Raven had to get the tide line from the Old One.

6. Raven felt that it would be _____

                communal   arduous   prudent

to listen to Mighty Spirit's words, so he did what he

was asked.

7. The Old One had a firm grip on the tide line. It was

_____ that she would not let go of it.

apparent   indebted   arduous

8. The Old One said, "Tell me what you're doing here!" But

Raven ignored all her _____ .

             bliss   demands   acquaintance

9. The Ancestors would be _____ to

           indebted   arduous   dissatisfied

Raven if he could get the Old One to let go of the tide line.

10. The tide would rush out and leave clams and crabs

_____ in seaweed on the shore.

prudent   dissatisfied   entwined

Write the answers to these questions. Use complete sentences.

11. What is a communal fire? _____

_____

12. What is an arduous task? Describe what it's like. _____

_____

RAVEN and the TIDES

A NATIVE AMERICAN LEGEND

retold by Barbara Adams

illustrated by Karen Perrins

CHARACTERS

NARRATOR	THE ANCESTORS (chorus)
STORYTELLER	MIGHTY SPIRIT
RAVEN	THE OLD ONE

NARRATOR: One cold winter night, ages ago, in a village on the Northwest Coast, families gathered around the communal fire to await the storyteller. When he emerged from his lodge, he had on a Raven mask. The children were quick to settle down, for they liked to hear the legends of Raven, the trickster.

STORYTELLER: Long before there were tides, the sea rose high along the edge of the land and stayed there. Because of this, the Ancestors could not gather clams and crabs unless they washed up on shore. This left the Ancestors hungry and dissatisfied with the sea's scant gifts. **1**

Stop and Think

1 Why are the ancestors dissatisfied?

The Ancestors are dissatisfied because _____

_____

_____

152

RAVEN: My belly is so empty that it is rumbling like thunder.

NARRATOR: The storyteller patted his belly and made the sound of thunder. Then he went on with the story.

THE ANCESTORS: We too are hungry and long for the taste of clams and crabs and other gifts that come from the sea.

RAVEN: I must think of a way to help the people—and myself.

STORYTELLER: But Raven was too hungry and tired, so he fell into a deep sleep. Taking pity on the Ancestors, Mighty Spirit spoke gently to Raven. ❷

Stop and Think

❷ What do you think Mighty Spirit will tell Raven?

I think Mighty Spirit will tell Raven _____

_____

_____

153

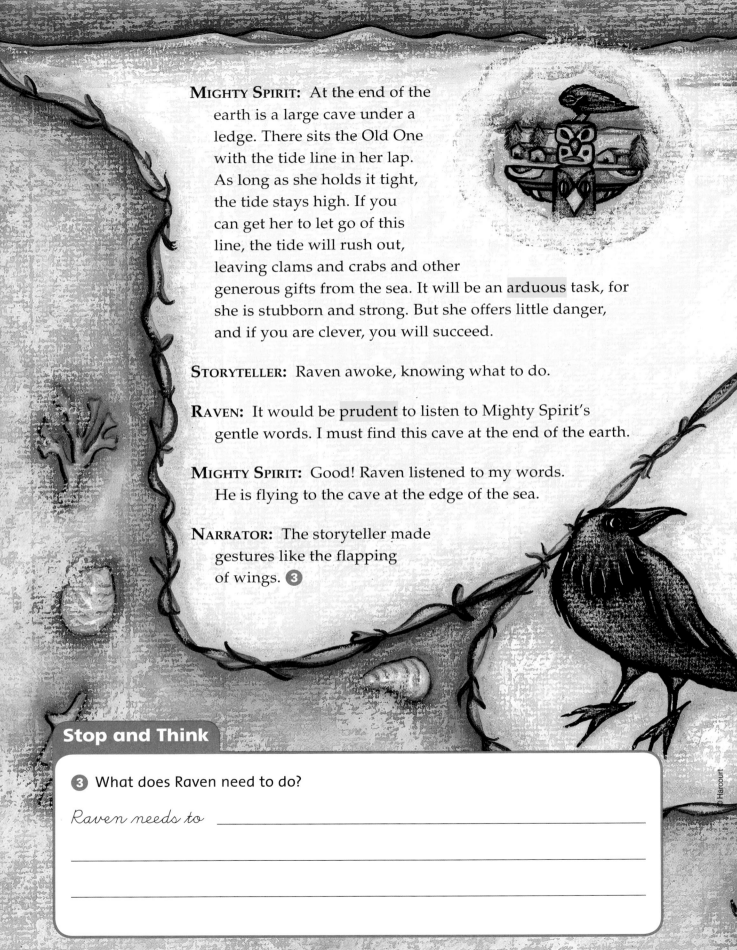

MIGHTY SPIRIT: At the end of the earth is a large cave under a ledge. There sits the Old One with the tide line in her lap. As long as she holds it tight, the tide stays high. If you can get her to let go of this line, the tide will rush out, leaving clams and crabs and other generous gifts from the sea. It will be an arduous task, for she is stubborn and strong. But she offers little danger, and if you are clever, you will succeed.

STORYTELLER: Raven awoke, knowing what to do.

RAVEN: It would be prudent to listen to Mighty Spirit's gentle words. I must find this cave at the end of the earth.

MIGHTY SPIRIT: Good! Raven listened to my words. He is flying to the cave at the edge of the sea.

NARRATOR: The storyteller made gestures like the flapping of wings. **3**

Stop and Think

3 What does Raven need to do?

Raven needs to _____

_____

_____

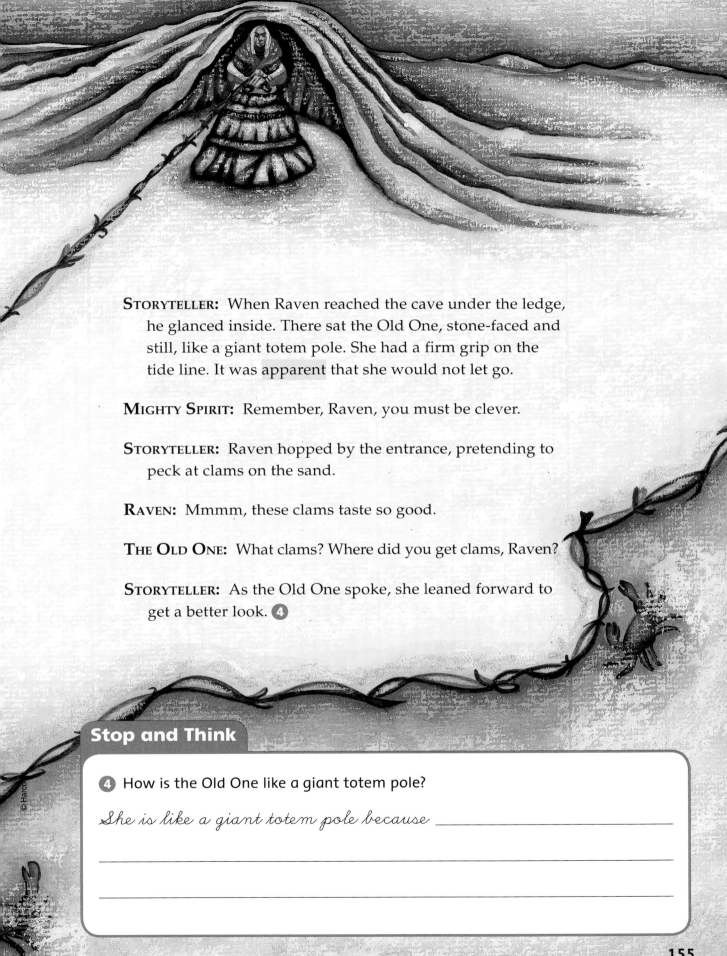

STORYTELLER: When Raven reached the cave under the ledge, he glanced inside. There sat the Old One, stone-faced and still, like a giant totem pole. She had a firm grip on the tide line. It was apparent that she would not let go.

MIGHTY SPIRIT: Remember, Raven, you must be clever.

STORYTELLER: Raven hopped by the entrance, pretending to peck at clams on the sand.

RAVEN: Mmmm, these clams taste so good.

THE OLD ONE: What clams? Where did you get clams, Raven?

STORYTELLER: As the Old One spoke, she leaned forward to get a better look. ④

Stop and Think

④ How is the Old One like a giant totem pole?

She is like a giant totem pole because _____

_____

_____

155

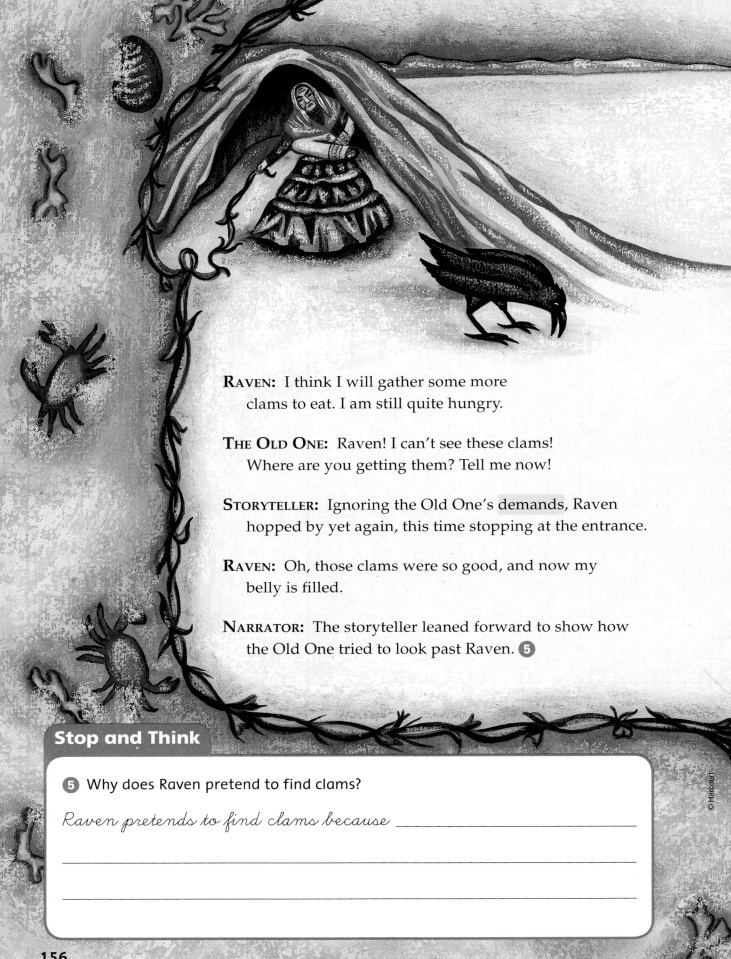

RAVEN: I think I will gather some more clams to eat. I am still quite hungry.

THE OLD ONE: Raven! I can't see these clams! Where are you getting them? Tell me now!

STORYTELLER: Ignoring the Old One's demands, Raven hopped by yet again, this time stopping at the entrance.

RAVEN: Oh, those clams were so good, and now my belly is filled.

NARRATOR: The storyteller leaned forward to show how the Old One tried to look past Raven. **5**

Stop and Think

5 Why does Raven pretend to find clams?

Raven pretends to find clams because _____

_____

_____

STORYTELLER: Trying to peer around the cave entrance, the Old One could no longer stay stationary. She let her grip slip on the tide line. Raven saw his chance, and grabbed the line out of her hand. The tide rushed out, leaving clams and crabs and other gifts from the sea entwined in seaweed on the shore.

THE OLD ONE: You sneaky bird!

STORYTELLER: Raven gathered clams and ate until he was hungry no more. His bliss lasted for just a while, and then he felt bad for the Old One. He carried some clams up to the Old One and dropped them in her lap.

THE OLD ONE: Mmmm, these clams are so tasty! Perhaps I could forget that you tricked me.

RAVEN: Now that the tide is low, I will return to the Ancestors, who will surely be indebted to me for bringing the tide. **6**

Stop and Think

6 What happens when Raven grabs the tide line?

When Raven grabs the tide line, _____

_____

_____

STORYTELLER: Later, as Raven slept, Mighty Spirit came to him again and spoke in a gentle way.

MIGHTY SPIRIT: Return to the Old One and give her this message . . .

STORYTELLER: So Raven went to speak to the Old One.

RAVEN: Mighty Spirit says that you must agree to let go of the tide line twice a day, so the Ancestors can gather clams and crabs and other generous gifts from the sea.

STORYTELLER: The Old One agreed, and that is why the tides come in and go out twice a day.

NARRATOR: The children were still awake when the storyteller finished, for they never tired of hearing the legends of Raven, the trickster. ⑦

Stop and Think

⑦ What natural event does this legend try to explain?

This legend tries to explain _____

_____

_____

Think Critically

1. What is the main problem in this story? How is it resolved? **PLOT**

The main problem is _____

_____

The problem is resolved when _____

_____

_____

2. Why do you think Raven decides to help the Ancestors? **CHARACTER**

I think Raven decides to help because _____

_____

_____

3. Why do you think the author uses a storyteller in this story?
AUTHOR'S PURPOSE

I think the author uses a storyteller because _____

_____

_____

_____

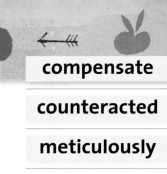

- compensate
- counteracted
- meticulously
- perfectionist
- petition
- precise
- regulates
- trial

Vocabulary

Build Robust Vocabulary

Read the selection and think about the meanings of the words in dark type.

In the 1600s, Isaac Newton was a leading scientist. Even as a child, he was interested in how things in our universe worked. As an adult, he tested his ideas in one **trial** case after another.

One of Newton's ideas explained how an object will travel on the same path at the same speed until it is **counteracted** by a second force. Newton also explained the force of gravity. It keeps planets in orbit around the sun and pulls objects on Earth toward the center. Newton showed how this same force of gravity between Earth and the Moon **regulates** the ocean tides.

Newton was a **perfectionist** in his experiments. He worked day and night for weeks at a time. He **meticulously** tested his ideas because he wanted his findings to be **precise**. He felt that great ideas alone could not **compensate** for errors in experiments.

At that time, you had to **petition** the Royal Society to publish your work. This group of scientists assisted other scientists by promoting their work. In 1687, the Society published a paper that explained all of Newton's ideas on gravity.

Write the answers to these questions. Use complete sentences.
The first one has been done for you.

1. How can you tell Isaac Newton was a **perfectionist**?

He was a perfectionist because he worked day and night for weeks at a time to

test his ideas.

2. Why did Newton **meticulously** test his ideas in **trial** cases?

_____

_____

3. What does it mean if an experiment is not **precise**?

_____

_____

4. How might an object be **counteracted** by another force?

_____

_____

5. According to Newton, what controls Earth's ocean tides?

_____

_____

6. When scientists **petition** the Society, what are they hoping for?

_____

_____

7. "Great ideas alone can't **compensate** for errors in experiments."
What does this mean?

_____

_____

After the Apple Fell

by Michelle Kirby
illustrated by Martin Haake

One day, Isaac Newton was sitting under a tree reading, when an apple fell on him, and his theory of gravity was born.

Have you heard this story? Well, it didn't happen quite like that. In fact, Newton spent twenty years working on his theories about gravity, and when his ideas were published in 1687, they changed our understanding of how the universe worked.

Isaac Newton was born on December 25, 1642, in Woolsthorpe, England. His father, a farmer, died before Isaac was born. When he was three years old, his mother married again and Isaac went to stay with his grandparents. **1**

Stop and Think

1 What is the point of view in this biography? How do you know?

The point of view is _____

_____

_____

162

From all accounts, Isaac was a quiet boy. He liked being alone and seemed to enjoy constructing things. Just for fun, Isaac made toy windmills, water clocks, and sundials.

It was clear that Isaac liked science, but he was expected to be a farmer like his father. His mother made him leave school and come home to work on the farm. However, Isaac wasn't a very good farmer—and he had little interest in growing things. He was more interested in the sun, stars, and planets surrounding his world. In fact, Isaac avoided his duties as a farmer. One time, he was found hiding in a hedge when he was supposed to be at the market! ❷

Stop and Think

❷ How do you think Isaac felt about leaving school?

I think Isaac felt _____

_____

_____

Isaac's former teacher recognized the boy's talent. He encouraged Issac's mother to send him to Trinity College at Cambridge University.

At Trinity College, young Newton studied the ideas of Aristotle, which were almost two thousand years old at the time! Aristotle believed that the planets rotated around Earth. Newton enjoyed reading the more recent works of Galileo and other scientists, who had different ideas about the solar system. One of these ideas was that the planets rotated around the sun. In 1665, Newton had to return home for two years, where he kept thinking about these new ideas. It was then that he really started to investigate gravity, light, and mathematics. ③

Stop and Think

③ What did Newton do in 1665?

In 1665, Newton _____

_____

_____

In 1667, Newton went back to Cambridge. By that time, he had developed his own ideas about gravity. Always a busy student, he moved on to study light and colors.

Scientists had been using prisms for a long time to experiment with light. A prism is a glass device that separates rays of light into a rainbow of different colors. At that time, people believed that prisms caused rays of light to change colors. The quality of 17th-century prisms was poor, so Newton had to find ways to compensate for their defects. He pasted black paper over a prism's chipped corners to get better results. After many experiments, Newton found that light was actually made of all different colors mixed together. **4**

Stop and Think

4 How did Newton change people's beliefs about light and prisms?

Newton _____

_____

_____

The Royal Society encouraged Newton's findings. The Royal Society was a group of important scientists. They tested new, promising ideas and assisted the inventors and scientists by promoting their work. One member, Robert Hooke, didn't get along with Newton. Newton's findings about light didn't agree with Hooke's ideas. However, many members of the Royal Society were still impressed with Newton, and in 1672, they asked Newton to join them.

When Newton first pointed out his ideas on gravity, Hooke publicly took credit for giving Newton these ideas. Newton was so annoyed and upset that he didn't publish any of his ideas for a long time. **5**

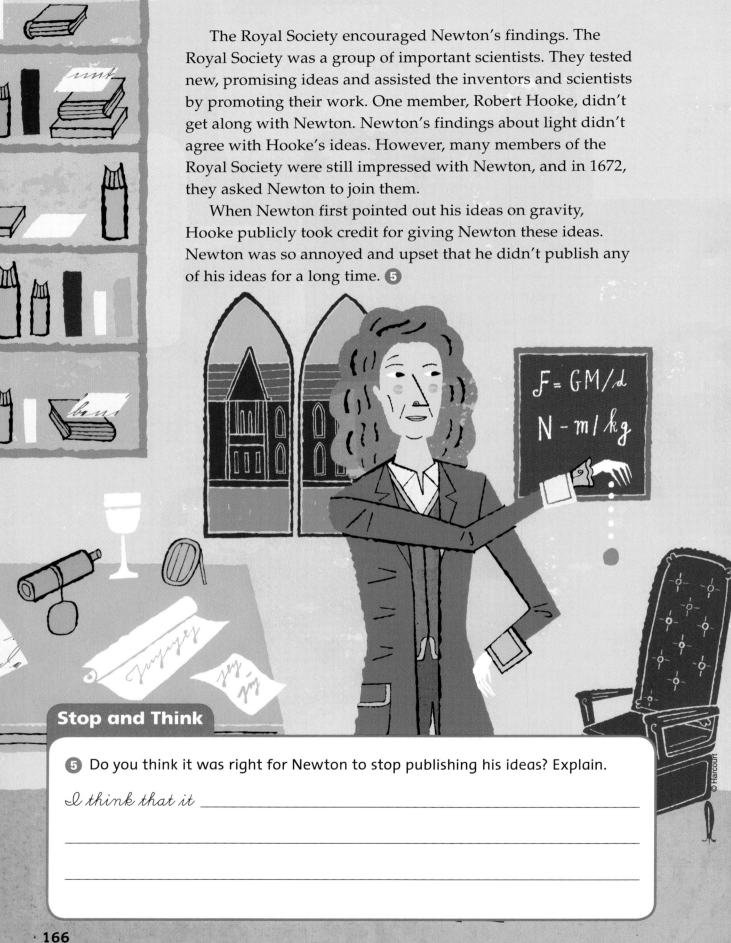

$$F = GM/d$$
$$N - m/kg$$

Stop and Think

5 Do you think it was right for Newton to stop publishing his ideas? Explain.

I think that it _____

_____

_____

Still, Newton didn't stop working on his ideas about gravity. He worked very hard and meticulously tested his theories. As a perfectionist, Newton toiled day and night for weeks at a time on his experiments. He set up many trial cases to see how the force of gravity worked. He gathered precise data using a form of mathematics he had created twenty years before called calculus. In 1687, Newton finished a paper on his findings. This amazing work explained all of his ideas on gravity.

His friend, Edmond Halley, realized the importance of Newton's work. Halley decided to petition the Royal Society to publish Newton's ideas. **6**

Stop and Think

6 How do you think other scientists will feel about Newton's paper?

I think other scientists will feel _____

_____

_____

Newton's paper explained the forces that make up our universe. For example, Newton said that an object will travel on the same path at the same speed until counteracted by a second force. Newton also explained how the force that keeps planets in orbit around the sun pulls objects on Earth toward the center, such as an apple falling from a tree. And he showed how this same force of gravity between Earth and the Moon regulates the ocean tides.

Newton's ideas explained so much about how our world works, and he invented the math to back up his ideas. Today, these methods and ideas are still used in the study of our universe. **7**

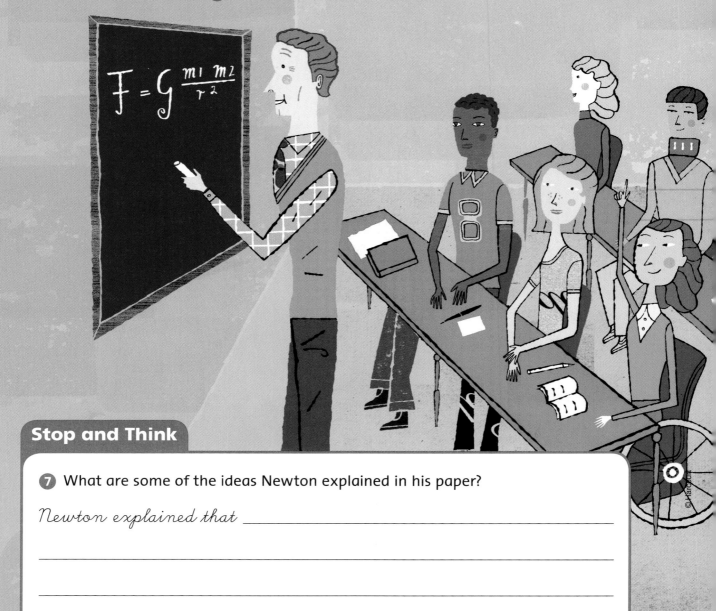

$$F = G \frac{m_1 \, m_2}{r^2}$$

Stop and Think

7 What are some of the ideas Newton explained in his paper?

Newton explained that _____

_____

_____

Think Critically

1. What important events led to the publication of Newton's paper on gravity? Fill in the chart with the order of events. SEQUENCE

First
In 1665, Newton began to study gravity.

Next
In 1667,

Then
In 1672,

Finally
In 1687,

2. What effect did Newton's ideas have on our understanding of the universe? CAUSE AND EFFECT

Newton's ideas caused _____

_____

_____

_____

3. What interesting facts have you learned about Isaac Newton? MAIN IDEA AND DETAILS

I have learned that _____

_____

_____

_____

contortions
distraction
faint
foresight
grimy
publicize
testimony

Vocabulary

Build Robust Vocabulary

Write the Vocabulary Word that completes each sentence in the diary. The first one has been done for you.

Monday

Flyers have been tacked up to **(1)** _____ publicize _____ the upcoming drama contest. When I told the others about my crazy plan to win the contest, Paul had a grin on his face that I almost didn't see. But that **(2)** _____ grin told me that he was interested in this plan.

We all agreed to have little kids act in our play, "The Three Little Pigs." We had to ask their parents to allow them to take part in the play. All the parents agreed. They were just glad to have any **(3)** _____ that would keep their toddlers occupied.

Saturday

Our attempt to make the set for the play didn't get off to a good start. Paul got a stick glued to his back by mistake. He twisted himself into **(4)** _____ trying to reach it and pull it off. Lin had to help him. Paul said, "I'll use this in my

(5) _____ to support the fact that the little pig should have made his house of bricks." I giggled at the idea of a brick glued to Paul's back.

By the time we finished making the set, we were

(6) _____ and needed to get cleaned up. We were lucky that Lin had the **(7)** _____ to bring soap and cleaning supplies.

© Harcourt

The Three Little ~~Pigs~~ Kids

by Susan Blackaby

illustrated by Gina Capaldi

The annual Children's Drama Contest in Carson's Creek had to be the most difficult contest to win. Every year, kids from across the town came to the small auditorium to judge the plays. But these were no ordinary kids. They were the most difficult critics in the world.

At first, the contest was a light-hearted one, with people acting out different folktales for the children's enjoyment. But at some point, the kids decided to control the whole show. The success of a play depended on the looks on the kids' faces. If they giggled, it was a hit! If they yawned, it was a flop. **1**

Stop and Think

1 What makes the drama contest so difficult to win?

The contest is so difficult to win because _kids are hard_
cridicts

©Harcourt

One year, the sixth-grade class decided to win this difficult contest. But they just couldn't figure out how to do it.

"We need to try something new and different," said Paul as he sat with his pals at the town's diner.

"I know, but what can we do?" muttered Lin. "Everything's been done, and those kids are expert judges!"

"Wait—I have an idea," said Tina, scribbling notes on a napkin. "If we can get some little kids to participate in our play, maybe it will cause the critics to relax a bit."

"What about your little sister?" Dawn asked Lin. "Maybe she could be in the play along with her friends." **2**

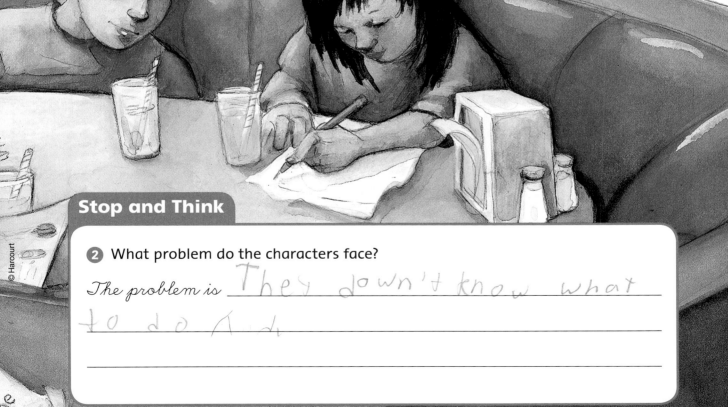

Stop and Think

2 What problem do the characters face?

The problem is _They down't know what to do nd_

Lin paused for a minute, thinking of her little sister's talent for making mischief. Considering this, the new plan seemed doubtful. "Do you think this will work?" she asked with a skeptical look.

"I think it sounds nuts," Paul replied, a faint grin on his face. "But I know a thing or two about little kids, so I think I can handle them." **3**

Stop and Think

3 What point of view does the author use in this story? How do you know?

The author uses _____

_____

_____

© Harcourt

The next day, the four directors had rounded up a small number of toddlers to act in "The Three Little Pigs." Lin's three-year-old sister, Lili, would play the wolf. As the kids rehearsed, their parents sat on the sidelines and watched with interest. They were clearly glad for any distraction that would keep their toddlers occupied for a while.

The first rehearsal was a disaster, but after several days the kids had worked out a decent play. Tina would narrate the play, while Paul would direct the kids around the stage. Dawn and Lin would whisper the lines to the kids.

Finally, they decided to publicize their play for the contest. They tacked up a handmade flyer on the window of the diner. ❹

Stop and Think

❹ How do you think the play will go? Why do you think so?

I think the play will ___Go great_____

_____

_____

© Harcourt

On the day of the play, Lin could tell that the audience was going to be the most difficult one in years. Seven-year-old Sarah Barnes sat in the front row, her arms folded across her chest. Lin sometimes babysat Sarah, and always had a hard time getting her to do anything fun. She seemed to have a permanent frown on her face, too.

Just before the play, Paul had the foresight to fill his pockets with crackers and other treats that might keep the little performers happy. The kids' parents leaned against the walls, holding their cameras. **5**

Stop and Think

5 How would you describe Sarah Barnes?

Sarah Barnes is _____

_____

_____

At first, the play got off to a rocky start because Lili was scared of the dark auditorium. But when Paul started handing her crackers, she followed his lead.

Then, in the middle of the play, four-year-old Patrick decided he wanted to be a dog, not a pig.

"Ruff, ruff!" he barked, crawling around on the stage. Paul groaned, wishing he had some doggy treats.

Later, Lili became angry when her big blows didn't cause the house made of sticks to fall down. With a face grimy with crumbs and a mouth full of crackers, she huffed and puffed . . . and showered Paul with cracker crumbs. Paul's body went into contortions as he twisted and turned to avoid the blast of crumbs. **6**

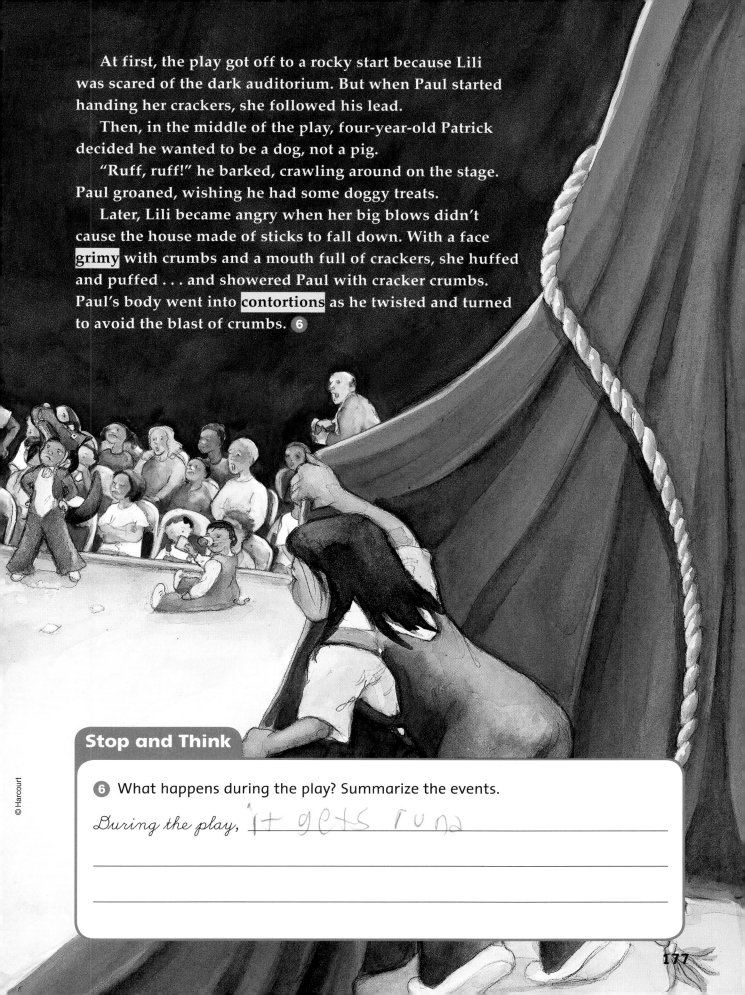

Stop and Think

6 What happens during the play? Summarize the events.

During the play, It gets runa

© Harcourt

Suddenly, the cast members heard strange sounds coming from the audience. The hard-to-please kids were having a difficult time controlling their giggles. Sarah Barnes was doubled over and laughing loudly.

Shocked, Paul looked at Dawn, who winked back. She whispered, "Keep going—we're making history here!"

After the contest, the directors treated the first-place winners to ice cream at the diner.

"Paul, you were a testimony to actors everywhere," announced Lin. "Despite cracker showers and barking pigs, you kept the show going!"

Just as he was about to protest, Paul looked down to see Patrick crawling up into his lap, preparing to give him a very sticky high-five. **7**

Stop and Think

7 What does Dawn mean when she says they are "making history"?

Dawn means that _____

_____

_____

© Harcourt

Think Critically

1. How is the conflict in the story resolved? Fill in the resolution box with your answer. CONFLICT/RESOLUTION

```
        ┌─────────────────┐
        │    Conflict     │
        └─────────────────┘
                 │
        ┌─────────────────┐
        │   Plot Events   │
        └─────────────────┘
                 │
┌───────────────────────────────────────┐
│               Resolution               │
│                                         │
│                                         │
│                                         │
└───────────────────────────────────────┘
```

2. How would the ending be different if the audience had not laughed? PLOT

If the audience had not laughed, _____

_____

_____

3. How does the author of this story make you smile? AUTHOR'S PURPOSE

The author makes me smile by _____

_____

_____

Vocabulary

beacon

clamor

coincidentally

disturbance

enthralled

marvel

objections

persisted

Build Robust Vocabulary

Write the Vocabulary Word that completes each sentence in the newspaper articles. The first one has been done for you.

DAILY NEWS   SECTION C

Ferris Wheel Is a Hit

by Will Dearborn

Sunday, July 2, 1893

The **(1)** _____**clamor**_____ of the crowds

reached a fever pitch Saturday at the World's Fair in Jackson Park.

The public was thrilled and **(2)** _____

by the amazing sight of a huge wheel

reaching into the sky.

The wheel was made by George Ferris.

Its ring of twinkling lights can be seen

from miles away. The wheel serves as a

(3) _____ of light

that leads people to the fun that awaits

them at the fair.

Waiting in line takes up a lot of time, but those who have

(4) _____ said they were not

disappointed. Riders will **(5)** _____ at

the amazing view from the top.

DAILY NEWS   SECTION C

Ferris Wheel Gets a Spin

by Will Dearborn

Monday, July 10, 1893

On Sunday, Ferris's wheel caused quite a stir at the World's Fair, and, **(6)** _____ so did the weather. It was a hot day, but no one had any

(7) _____ to the heat as they waited to ride the wheel into the sky. Then a big storm came up near the fairgrounds just as riders got on the big wheel. But the **(8)** _____ caused by the strong winds did not dampen the spirits of the riders. "It was a wild ride!" said Lester Harris of Evanston. "I think the storm gave me a free spin on the wheel!"

181

the Big Wheel that Could

by David Neufeld

illustrated by Bob Dombrowski

In 1892, the fast-growing city of Chicago was in the middle of constructing a World's Fair at Jackson Park. George Washington Ferris had a plan. He would build a huge wheel with spokes. The wheel would carry 2,000 riders at a time to a height of 264 feet—as high as the highest skyscraper in Chicago. Everyone would marvel at the amazing sight.

Some said the wheel couldn't be made. Ferris needed more steel than any one steel mill could make. Coincidentally, Ferris was a steel mill inspector for all the mills in the nation. Twelve different steel mills would make the parts he needed, but the parts had to fit just right when they were combined. ①

Stop and Think

① Why do some people think the wheel can't be made?

Some people think it can't be made because _____

_____

_____

182

Engineers determined that the two towers that held the wheel, each 140 feet tall, should be strong and stable. The ground under Jackson Park was sandy, a substance not regarded as very stable. However, Ferris persisted in making his idea work. In the middle of a freezing winter, his company of workers broke through three feet of frost and drove dozens of wood posts thirty feet into the sand. A concrete base was poured around the posts to keep them in place.

The huge wheel would turn on a gigantic steel axle that was larger than any company had ever lifted. This 143,000-pound axle needed to be lifted 140 feet from the ground! **2**

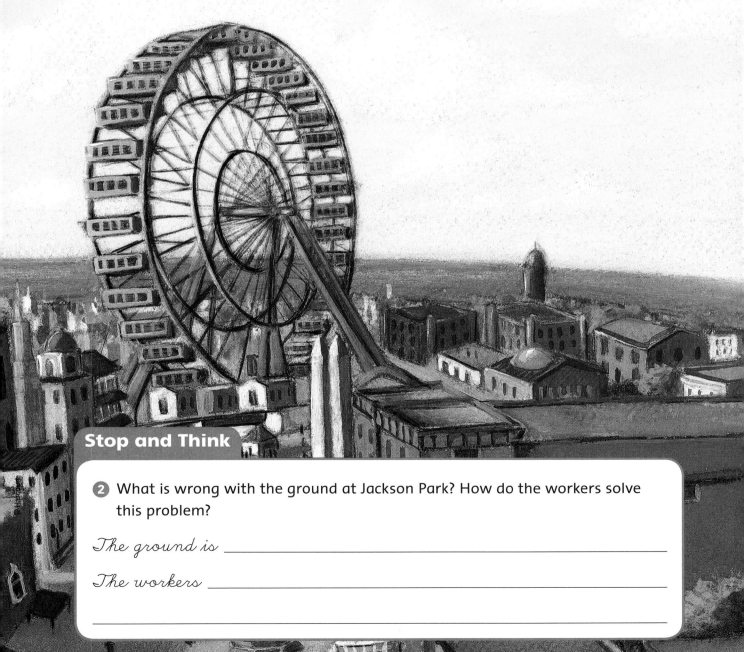

Stop and Think

2 What is wrong with the ground at Jackson Park? How do the workers solve this problem?

The ground is _____

The workers _____

_____

183

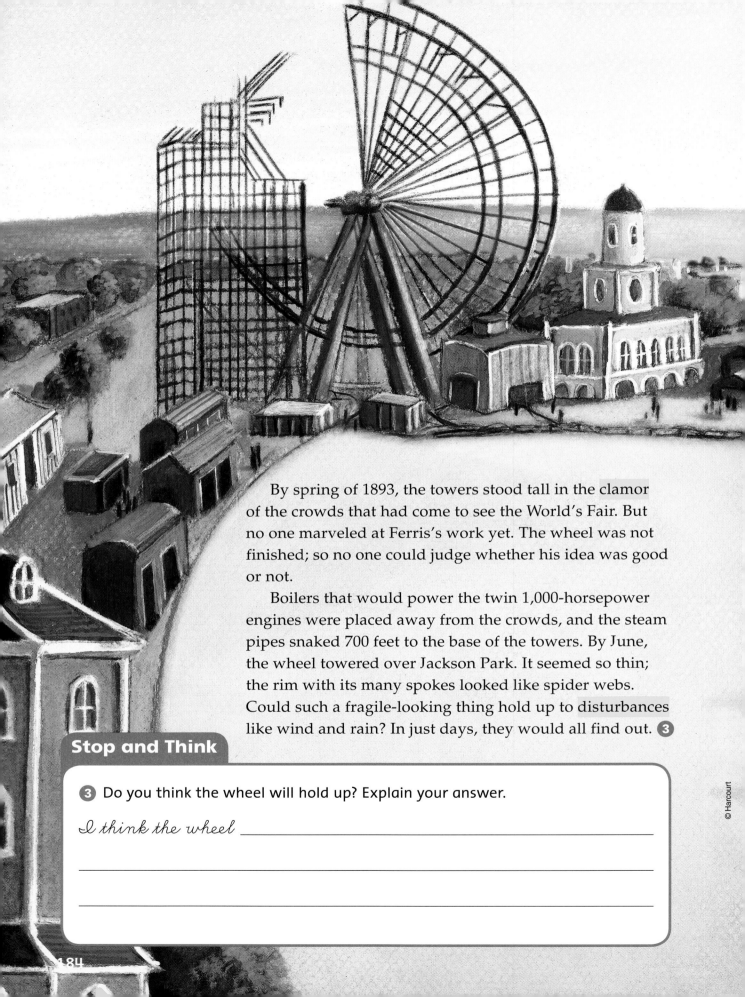

By spring of 1893, the towers stood tall in the clamor of the crowds that had come to see the World's Fair. But no one marveled at Ferris's work yet. The wheel was not finished; so no one could judge whether his idea was good or not.

Boilers that would power the twin 1,000-horsepower engines were placed away from the crowds, and the steam pipes snaked 700 feet to the base of the towers. By June, the wheel towered over Jackson Park. It seemed so thin; the rim with its many spokes looked like spider webs. Could such a fragile-looking thing hold up to disturbances like wind and rain? In just days, they would all find out. **3**

Stop and Think

3 Do you think the wheel will hold up? Explain your answer.

I think the wheel _____

_____

_____

© Harcourt

Very early on Friday, June 9, 1893, and one year late, the wheel took its first turn. The lead engineer nodded to the second engineer, and the second engineer pulled on the handle that let the steam into the engines. The twenty-ton chains began to turn.

Ferris, the genius behind the wheel, wasn't there to see his machine work. However, his wife was there in his place to witness the big event. She stood in amazement for the twenty minutes it took the enormous wheel to make its first full turn. **4**

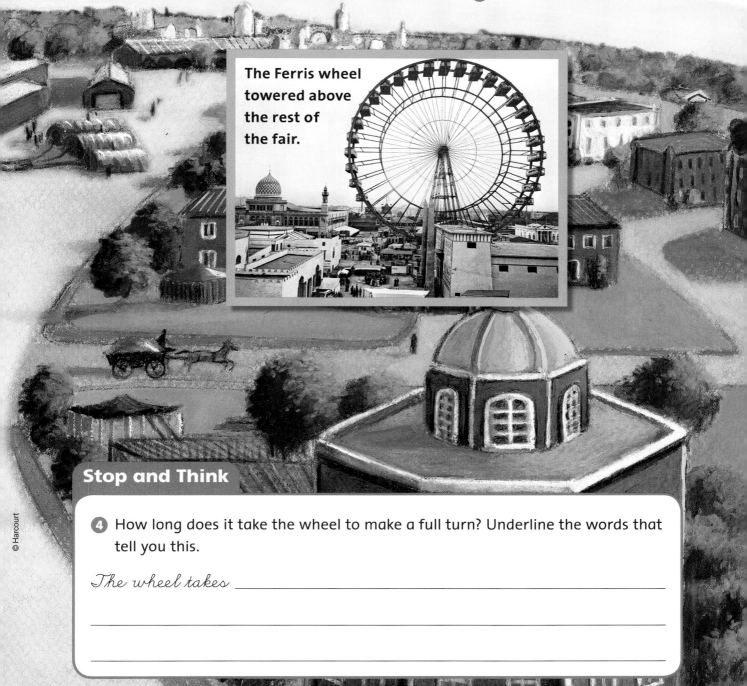

The Ferris wheel towered above the rest of the fair.

Stop and Think

4 How long does it take the wheel to make a full turn? Underline the words that tell you this.

The wheel takes _____

_____

_____

Over the next few weeks, thirty-six cars, thirteen tons each, were hung on the wheel. Up to sixty people could fit in each elegant car, so the wheel would have to hold over 300,000 pounds in passenger weight.

The day came when a small group of important visitors stepped aboard the first car. "I did not enter the car with the easiest feeling at heart," Ferris's partner, William Gronau, said. "Yet I could not refuse to take the trip. So I put on a bold face."

The car went up and stopped partway, and Gronau looked down to see that some eager first riders had boarded the empty cars behind his. This wasn't in the plan, but his objections were overshadowed by the clamor of the crowd. **5**

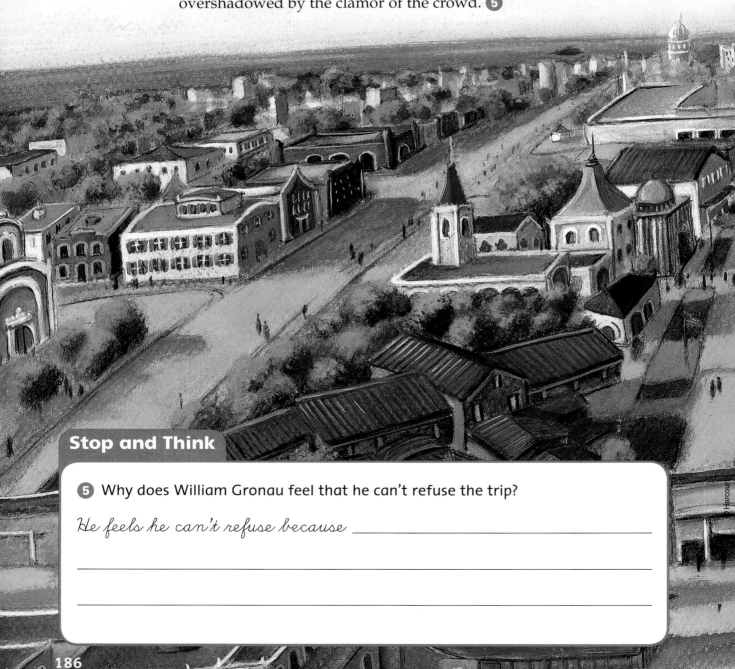

Stop and Think

5 Why does William Gronau feel that he can't refuse the trip?

He feels he can't refuse because _____

_____

_____

Harcourt

Gronau said later, "The sight is so inspiring, that all talk stopped." As their car came over the top and returned toward the earth, a few dozen bolts and nuts rattled onto the roof, but the wheel remained standing. The public was enthralled by the Ferris wheel, and they came again and again to ride the wheel into the sky.

The weather in July turned hot, and still people flocked to ride the Ferris wheel. At three p.m. on July 9, 1893, a swift storm rolled toward Jackson Park, causing everyone to scatter for shelter. Another ride was demolished, but the strong wind shook the wheel and its hundreds of riders just a little bit. **6**

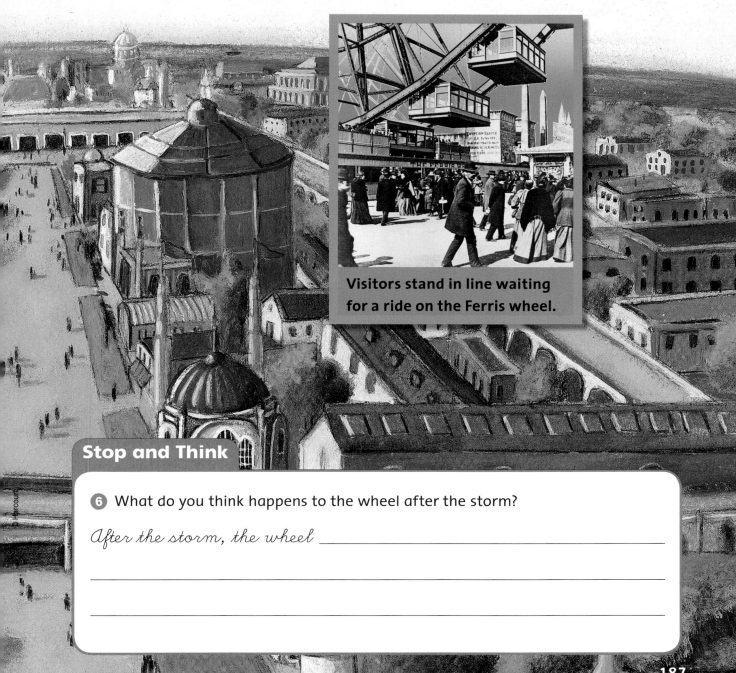

Visitors stand in line waiting for a ride on the Ferris wheel.

Stop and Think

6 What do you think happens to the wheel after the storm?

After the storm, the wheel _____

_____

_____

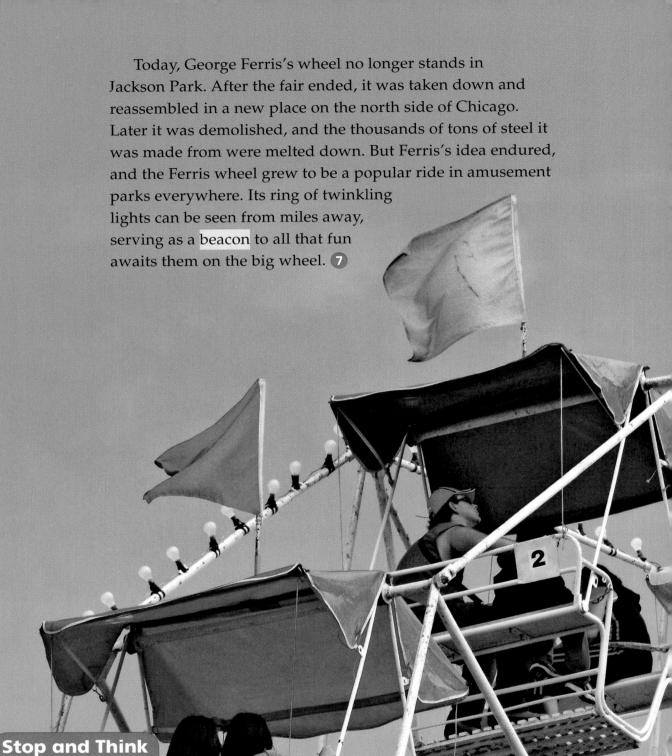

Today, George Ferris's wheel no longer stands in Jackson Park. After the fair ended, it was taken down and reassembled in a new place on the north side of Chicago. Later it was demolished, and the thousands of tons of steel it was made from were melted down. But Ferris's idea endured, and the Ferris wheel grew to be a popular ride in amusement parks everywhere. Its ring of twinkling lights can be seen from miles away, serving as a beacon to all that fun awaits them on the big wheel. 7

Stop and Think

7 How has Ferris's idea endured?

Ferris's idea has endured because _____

_____

_____

Think Critically

1. What do you learn about the first Ferris wheel? Write the main idea in the organizer. MAIN IDEA AND DETAILS

Detail	**Detail**	**Detail**
built in 1892	at World's Fair in Chicago	built by George Ferris

    Main Idea

2. Why do you think George Ferris wanted to build the huge wheel? CHARACTER

    I think he wanted to build it because _____

    _____

    _____

3. Why do you think the author wants you to know about the first Ferris wheel? AUTHOR'S PURPOSE

    I think he wants me to _____

    _____

    _____

189

abandoned

beloved

demolished

eager

humongous

neglected

severe

Vocabulary

Build Robust Vocabulary

Read the selection and think about the meanings of the words in dark type.

Redwoods are **humongous** trees that grow in northern California. In the two thousand or more years of a redwood's long life, it likely will overcome numerous fires, storms, and **severe** rains.

Only a few of the oldest redwoods have been left standing. In the past, logging companies cut down these trees for lumber. In the 1990s, they were **eager** to cut down redwood forests. The logging companies got permits that would have allowed these huge trees to be **demolished**.

Some felt that it was their duty to save these trees. One such person is Julia Hill. She felt that protecting the redwoods was a duty that should not be **neglected**.

When one California redwood was in danger of being cut down by a logging company, Julia Hill climbed that tree. She decided she wouldn't let anyone harm the **beloved** redwood.

No one could cut down the tree if Julia was in it, but if she **abandoned** the tree, it would be demolished. At first, she believed she would stay for only a few weeks, but Julia stayed in the tree for two years!

© Harcourt

Write the answers to these questions. Use complete sentences. The first one has been done for you.

1. If a tree is **humongous**, what is it like? Describe it.
   It's huge, very large, or gigantic.
   _____

2. What are **severe** rains like?
   _____
   _____

3. What were the logging companies **eager** to do?
   _____
   _____

4. What happens to a redwood when it is **demolished**?
   _____
   _____

5. What does it mean if someone **neglected** his or her duty?
   _____
   _____

6. In this selection, why is the redwood tree called the "**beloved** redwood"?
   _____
   _____

7. The tree was not **abandoned** by Julia. What does this mean?
   _____
   _____

Redwoods
Up Close and Personal!

by David Neufeld

When you see your first towering redwood tree, it's hard to believe that anything can grow that tall and that gigantic. In fact, some redwoods can grow as tall as 385 feet and are believed to be at least 3,000 years old. The trees grow in just a few forests in California, where the wet coastal climate suits them.

No one knows how long a giant redwood can exist. Its thick bark and ability to fight disease help these giants survive. Often, fires help the trees scatter their seeds. In some cases, a ring of new trees surrounds a burned-out stump. These ring trees likely sprouted after a fire demolished the older tree. **1**

Stop and Think

1 What do you learn about redwood trees?

I learn that _____

_____

_____

Some giant redwoods that have died are now tourist stops for travelers. A few redwoods have holes cut into their trunks so wide that you can drive a car in them for a thrill. Every day, **eager** drivers pay money to pose for a picture just as they exit the tree. Steel rods in the trees keep them standing. Cars can also drive onto Drive-On Tree, a **humongous** tree trunk that has been turned into a paved ramp. ➋

A tourist marvels at this hollowed-out redwood trunk.

Tourists drive inside a split tree trunk.

Stop and Think

➋ Do you think that these tourist stops are a good idea? Explain your answer.

I think that these tourist stops _____

_____

_____

Tree houses like this one line the Avenue of Giants, a roadway that passes by redwood tourist spots in California.

OPEN

Some redwoods have also become places where tourists can kick up their feet and rest for a while. World Famous Tree House is a hollow redwood with a light bulb suspended way up in the trunk of the tree. The bulb lights the inside of what might have been just an old tree neglected by time.

The Famous One Log House is one smart way to use an old tree trunk. Inside is a cozy bedroom for anyone who wants a house made out of only one piece of wood. Metal loops keep the house from falling apart, and a small roof keeps rain from dripping on guests. ③

Stop and Think

③ How are these two tourist stops alike? How are they different?

Here is how they are alike: _____

_____

Here is how they are different: _____

_____

© Harcourt

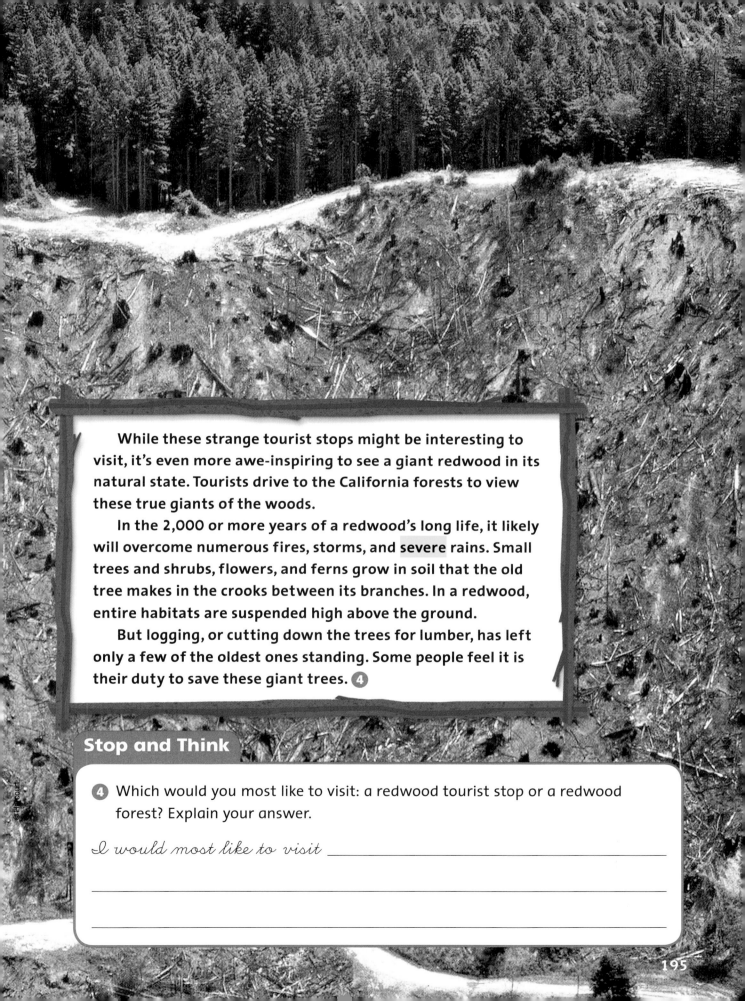

While these strange tourist stops might be interesting to visit, it's even more awe-inspiring to see a giant redwood in its natural state. Tourists drive to the California forests to view these true giants of the woods.

In the 2,000 or more years of a redwood's long life, it likely will overcome numerous fires, storms, and severe rains. Small trees and shrubs, flowers, and ferns grow in soil that the old tree makes in the crooks between its branches. In a redwood, entire habitats are suspended high above the ground.

But logging, or cutting down the trees for lumber, has left only a few of the oldest ones standing. Some people feel it is their duty to save these giant trees. **4**

Stop and Think

4 Which would you most like to visit: a redwood tourist stop or a redwood forest? Explain your answer.

I would most like to visit _____

_____

_____

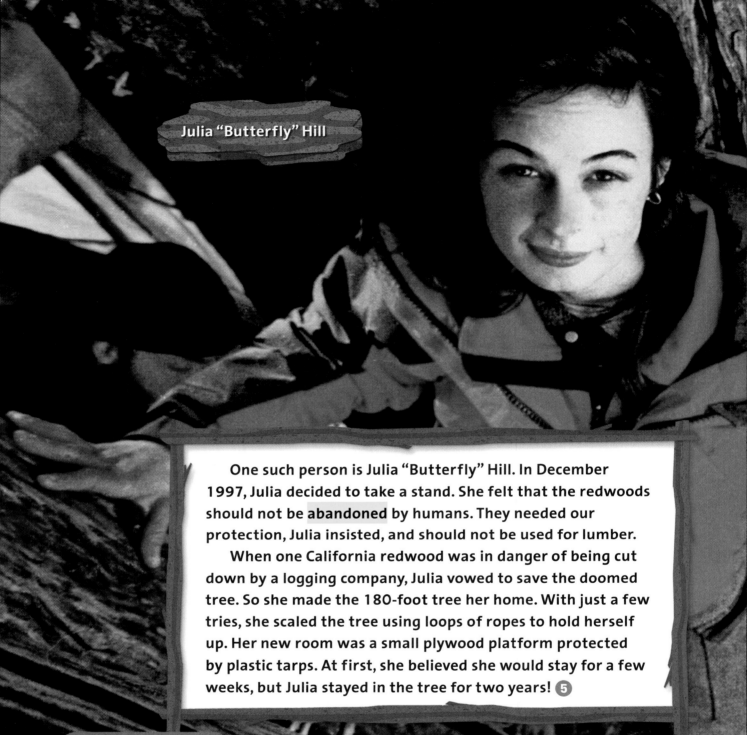

Julia "Butterfly" Hill

One such person is Julia "Butterfly" Hill. In December 1997, Julia decided to take a stand. She felt that the redwoods should not be **abandoned** by humans. They needed our protection, Julia insisted, and should not be used for lumber.

When one California redwood was in danger of being cut down by a logging company, Julia vowed to save the doomed tree. So she made the 180-foot tree her home. With just a few tries, she scaled the tree using loops of ropes to hold herself up. Her new room was a small plywood platform protected by plastic tarps. At first, she believed she would stay for a few weeks, but Julia stayed in the tree for two years! **5**

Stop and Think

5 Why does Julia decide to live in the tree?

Julia decides to live in the tree because _____

_____

_____

© Harcourt

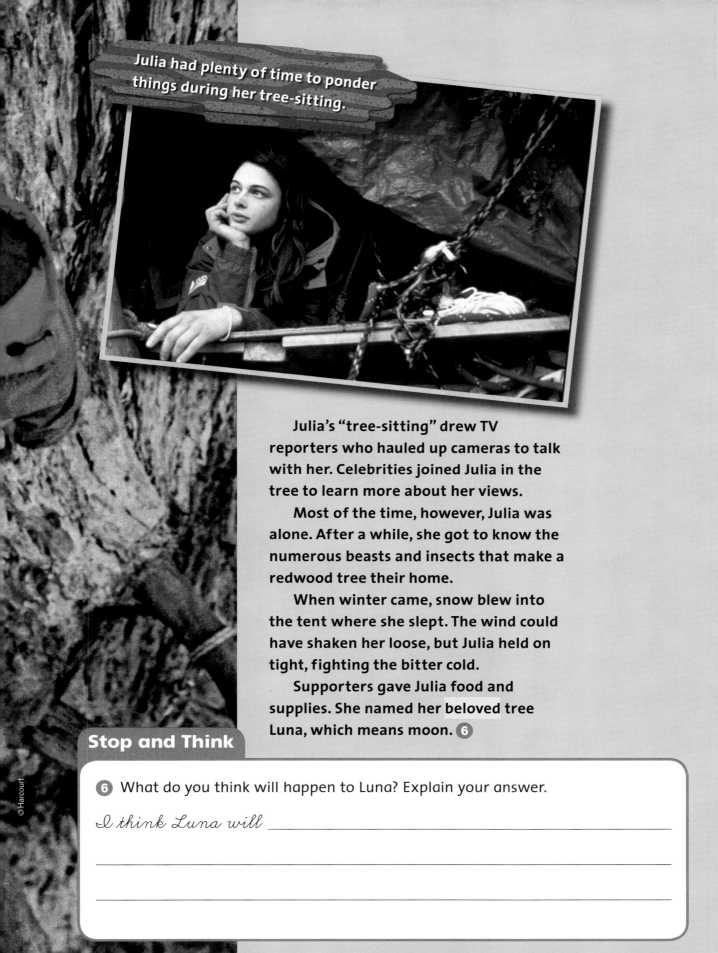

Julia had plenty of time to ponder things during her tree-sitting.

Julia's "tree-sitting" drew TV reporters who hauled up cameras to talk with her. Celebrities joined Julia in the tree to learn more about her views.

Most of the time, however, Julia was alone. After a while, she got to know the numerous beasts and insects that make a redwood tree their home.

When winter came, snow blew into the tent where she slept. The wind could have shaken her loose, but Julia held on tight, fighting the bitter cold.

Supporters gave Julia food and supplies. She named her beloved tree Luna, which means moon. **6**

Stop and Think

6 What do you think will happen to Luna? Explain your answer.

I think Luna will _____

_____

_____

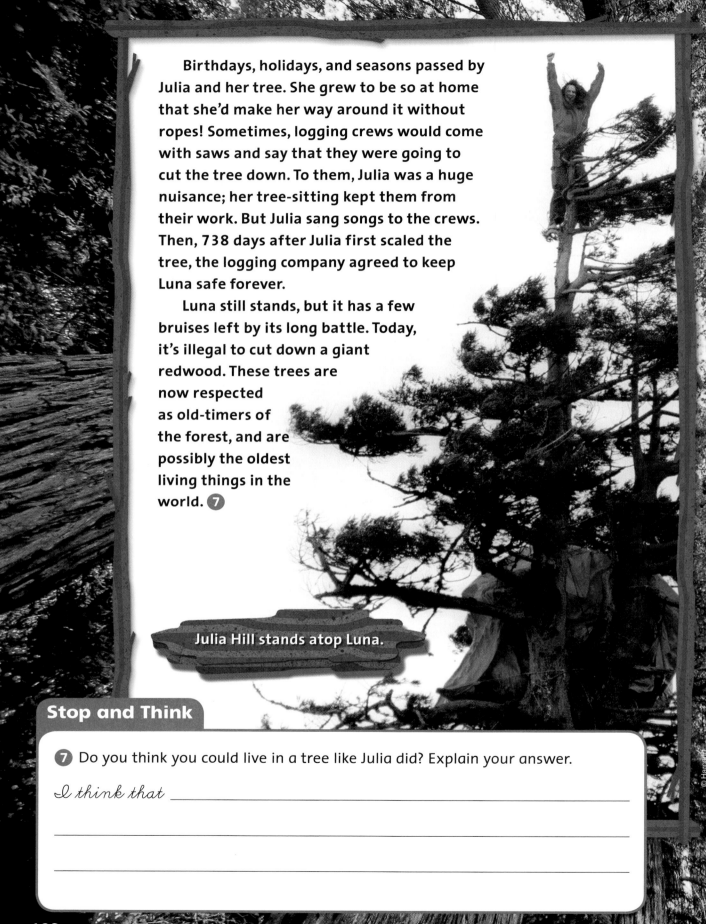

Birthdays, holidays, and seasons passed by Julia and her tree. She grew to be so at home that she'd make her way around it without ropes! Sometimes, logging crews would come with saws and say that they were going to cut the tree down. To them, Julia was a huge nuisance; her tree-sitting kept them from their work. But Julia sang songs to the crews. Then, 738 days after Julia first scaled the tree, the logging company agreed to keep Luna safe forever.

Luna still stands, but it has a few bruises left by its long battle. Today, it's illegal to cut down a giant redwood. These trees are now respected as old-timers of the forest, and are possibly the oldest living things in the world. **7**

Julia Hill stands atop Luna.

Stop and Think

7 Do you think you could live in a tree like Julia did? Explain your answer.

I think that _____

_____

_____

© Harcourt

Think Critically

1. Why are giant redwoods so awe-inspiring? **GENERALIZE**

Giant redwoods are so awe-inspiring because _____

_____

_____

_____

2. What is the main thing you would tell others about Julia Hill?
   MAIN IDEA AND DETAILS

Detail	**Detail**	**Detail**
lived in a redwood tree for two years	*got food and supplies from supporters*	*talked with others about her views*

Main Idea

3. How do you think the author feels about protecting the
   redwoods? **AUTHOR'S VIEWPOINT**

I think the author feels that _____

_____

_____

Build Robust Vocabulary

Write the word that best completes each sentence. The first one has been done for you.

1. Puppetry _____**aficionados**_____ from all over the

        tractions   aficionados   objections

world are at the Festival of Puppets.

2. The festival is the _____ of puppeteer

        brainchild   unison   traction

Manfred Cooper. He wanted to share the world of puppetry

with others.

3. At the festival, puppeteers _____

        commemorate   neglect   wage

battles to see who has the best puppet.

4. Thousands of years ago, _____

        avid   astute   utilitarian

puppets served a useful purpose.

5. Experts believe the first puppets were used to

_____ the gods

wage   commemorate   abandon

in ancient Egypt and Greece.

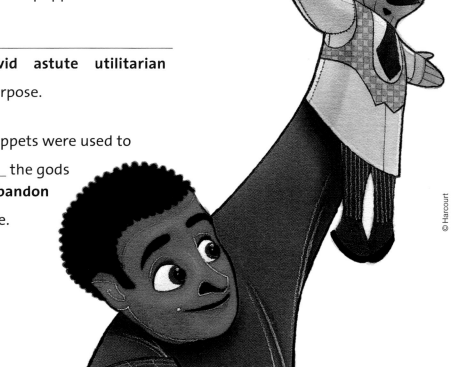

© Harcourt

6. There are _____ puppeteers at the

       avid   utilitarian   conventional

festival who like to talk about puppets all the time.

7. One puppeteer explains how _____

                 unison   traction   aficionado

is used to pull the strings on Japanese Bunraku puppets.

8. Most children around the world have seen a

_____ hand puppet. This

utilitarian   avid   conventional

common type of puppet is also on display.

9. In a different puppet show, two puppets dance

in _____ to celebrate

 traction   aficionados   unison

the Hopi corn ceremony.

10. Making two puppets dance like this is difficult. The

puppeteer must be very _____.

          conventional   astute   utilitarian

Write the answers to these questions. Use complete sentences.

11. What is a puppet aficionado?

_____

_____

12. In ancient times, what were utilitarian puppets used for?

_____

_____

Puppets
Around the World

by Michelle Kirby
illustrated by Thomas Thesen

CHARACTERS

TAYLOR BRADFORD, TV reporter   FLETCH PETERS

JESS CARVER, TV reporter   AKINA YOSHIDA

MANFRED COOPER   SANDRA DIAZ

CHORUS   TOM BAXTER

TAYLOR BRADFORD: Good afternoon! I'm Taylor Bradford with *Kid News*, reporting live from the tenth annual Festival of Puppets. Puppetry aficionados from all over the world are here to show off their puppets and to try for some of the many prizes.

JESS CARVER: This event is the brainchild of puppeteer Manfred Cooper. Mr. Cooper wanted to share the world of puppetry with others, so he began writing and performing children's puppet theater around the world. I'm pleased that Manfred is here to talk with us today. ❶

Stop and Think

❶ What information do you think Manfred Cooper will share?

I think Manfred Cooper will share _____

_____

_____

MANFRED COOPER: Thank you. When people think of puppets, they think of simple sock or stick puppets that children might enjoy. But some puppets can be quite complex and require the work of skilled artists.

JESS CARVER: So puppets aren't just for kids?

CHORUS: What? Puppets aren't just for kids?

MANFRED COOPER: Nope, puppetry is an art form that dates back thousands of years. In fact, the first puppets were utilitarian, serving a useful purpose in these early cultures. Experts believe these first puppets were used in ceremonies to commemorate the gods in ancient Egypt and Greece. Since then, puppetry has become an important part of storytelling in almost all cultures. **2**

Stop and Think

2 How does Manfred Cooper feel about puppetry?

Manfred Cooper feels that _____

_____

_____

JESS CARVER: How interesting! Thank you for your time, Mr. Cooper. Let's check out some of the puppets here today. Mr. Peters, your sign reads *Flat Rod Puppets*. Can you tell us about those?

FLETCH PETERS: Sure. Flat rod puppets are used to make shadows. You know, these were popular in China. Candles or torches were placed behind a silk screen and the puppets were held up to create shadows. The audience saw only the shadows, not the puppets.

JESS CARVER: What a cool concept! Let's go now to Taylor and see what she's discovered. ❸

Stop and Think

❸ How do flat rod puppets work?

Flat rod puppets _____

_____

_____

TAYLOR BRADFORD: Jess, I'm here with Akina Yoshida, who has come all the way from Japan to show her puppets. Do you have a second to talk to us, Ms. Yoshida?

AKINA YOSHIDA: Of course! I'm an avid puppeteer, so I like talking to anyone about puppets. These are Japanese Bunraku puppets. As you can see, they have strings attached at the top, the arms, and the legs.

TAYLOR BRADFORD: Wow! You must need a lot of traction to pull the strings on these mega-puppets.

AKINA YOSHIDA: Yes, it takes the strength of three puppeteers to control just one puppet.

CHORUS: They look so lifelike and real! 4

Stop and Think

4 What can you tell about Bunraku puppets?

I can tell that Bunraku puppets _____

_____

_____

AKINA YOSHIDA: Puppets have long been part of Japanese culture and were first used in worship ceremonies. This particular type of puppet has been around since the 1600s. Over time, more people wanted to be entertained. Puppeteers traveled around Japan performing in puppet theaters. Plays written during this time were often about regular people and their lives.

CHORUS: Just like TV shows—but with puppets on a stage!

TAYLOR BRADFORD: Thank you, Ms. Yoshida, for demonstrating your fascinating puppets. Now, back to Jess. **5**

Stop and Think

5 How are Japanese puppet theaters and today's TV shows alike?

They are alike because _____

_____

_____

Jess Carver: I'm talking to Sandra Diaz, who has the more conventional hand puppets that many children have seen. Tell us about this puppet that looks like a knight.

Sandra Diaz: It *is* a knight. The body is hollow so my hand can fit inside and control its movements. This knight can even wage battles with other knight puppets, like this.

Chorus: Wow—careful, Jess!

Jess Carver: Are hand puppets the oldest kind of puppet?

Sandra Diaz: Well, no one knows for sure. Early paintings in China show evidence of hand puppets, so we do know they have been around a long time.

Jess Carver: Thanks, Ms. Diaz, for sharing your fantastic puppets with us! Taylor? **6**

Stop and Think

6 Why are hand puppets more conventional?

They are more conventional because _____

_____

_____

Taylor Bradford: What an elaborate string puppet you have there, Mr. Baxter! Tell us about it.

Tom Baxter: This is a marionette of the Butterfly Maiden, a Kachina doll that is part of Native American Hopi culture. In this puppet corn ceremony, two marionettes dance in unison to music, then pretend to grind the corn. See, it moves when you pull the strings. It's all in the wrist.

Taylor Bradford: That sounds difficult. It must require the work of some astute puppeteers.

Tom Baxter: Yes, it sure does.

Taylor Bradford: Wow—puppets are an important part of history and culture all over the world! This wraps up our episode of *Kid News* for this week. Thanks for tuning in! ➐

Stop and Think

➐ Do you think puppets are an important part of history and culture? Explain.

I think that puppets _____

_____

_____

Think Critically

1. **How are the puppets alike? How are they different?**
   COMPARE AND CONTRAST

   Here is how they are alike: _____

   _____

   Here is how they are different: _____

   _____

2. **What have you learned about the history of puppetry?**
   MAIN IDEA AND DETAILS

   I have learned that _____

   _____

   _____

3. **How do you think the author feels about puppetry?**
   AUTHOR'S PURPOSE

   I think the author feels _____

   _____

   _____

   _____

209

banned

ethics

influenced

logic

modern

promote

pursuit

urges

Vocabulary

Build Robust Vocabulary

Write the Vocabulary Word that completes each sentence. The first one has been done for you.

In 776 B.C., the first Olympic games we know about took place in Greece. The Olympics helped to

(1) _____promote_____ sportsmanship and fairness. The Greeks had rules based on their sense of right and wrong. The athletes upheld those Greek **(2)** _____ .

The Olympic games of long ago were quite different from the Olympics of today. The ancient Greeks

(3) _____ women from participating. They didn't think women had the right body type. Sadly, their faulty **(4)** _____ prevented women from competing in athletic events for centuries.

© Harcourt

The (5) _____ Olympic games have more events than the ancient games. Now there are both summer and winter games. Athletes participate in snow sports during the winter games. Some summer games focus on water sports, such as swimming and diving. Athletes in all sports train hard in their (6) _____ of winning a gold medal.

Today, the Olympic committee in each country (7) _____ top athletes to try out for the games. People feel a sense of pride when an athlete from their country wins a medal.

The Olympics carry on many traditions from the past. Today's games are still (8) _____ by athletes from centuries ago.

Write the Vocabulary Word that best completes the synonym web.

9.

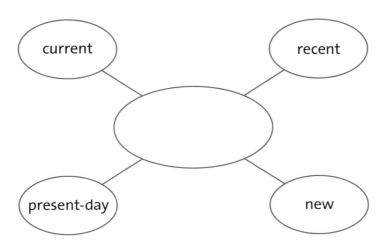

current

recent

present-day

new

The Olympics
Yesterday and Today

by Linda Lott

The year is 2004, and a huge crowd pours into Ancient Olympia Stadium in Athens, Greece. As the athletes warm up, spectators snap photos from the stands.

Soon, it's time for the women's shot put event to start. The first athlete prepares to hurl the ball as far as she can, and then she lets go of it. As she watches the ball fly through the air, she silently urges it to go farther, farther.

Will she win the gold medal? Even if she doesn't win, the athlete can be proud because she's taking part in a historic event in a historic place. ❶

Stop and Think

❶ What can you tell about this selection from its title?

I can tell that this selection _____

_____

_____

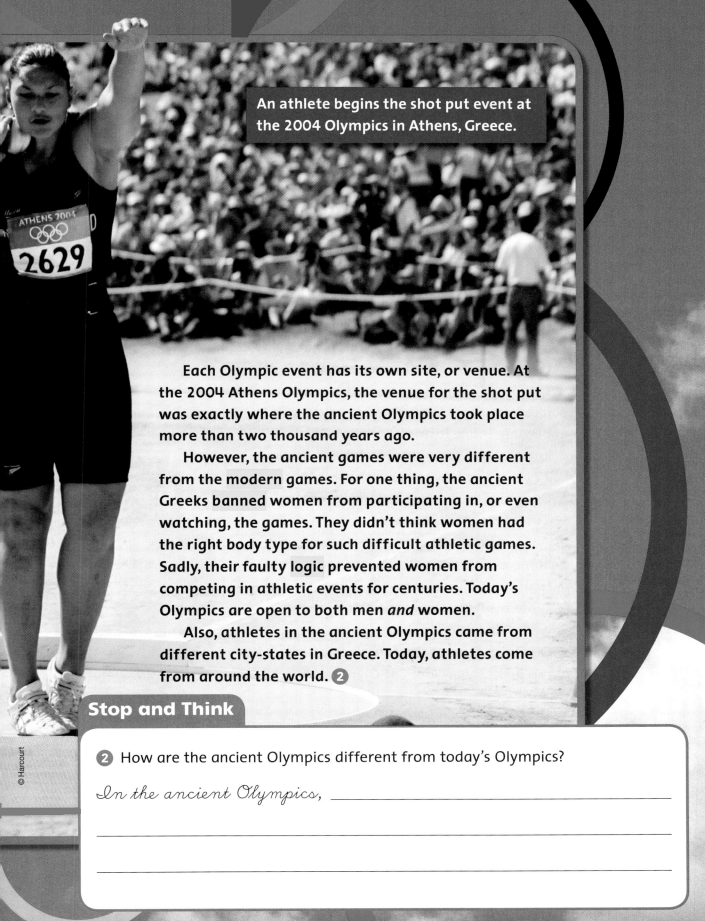

An athlete begins the shot put event at the 2004 Olympics in Athens, Greece.

Each Olympic event has its own site, or venue. At the 2004 Athens Olympics, the venue for the shot put was exactly where the ancient Olympics took place more than two thousand years ago.

However, the ancient games were very different from the modern games. For one thing, the ancient Greeks banned women from participating in, or even watching, the games. They didn't think women had the right body type for such difficult athletic games. Sadly, their faulty logic prevented women from competing in athletic events for centuries. Today's Olympics are open to both men *and* women.

Also, athletes in the ancient Olympics came from different city-states in Greece. Today, athletes come from around the world. **2**

Stop and Think

2 How are the ancient Olympics different from today's Olympics?

In the ancient Olympics, _____

_____

_____

In the ancient Olympics, the winner didn't take home a gold medal. He was crowned with a wreath.

No one knows exactly when the Olympics began. Thousands of years ago, Greek athletes may have competed in small games that were like fairs. Over time, these physical games became more formal. The first Olympics we know about took place in Athens around 776 B.C., but it was much shorter than today's Olympics. There was just one event, a 200-meter running race.

Soon, more Olympic events were added. Some events were harsh and seem cruel to us now. There were difficult fights, and some athletes even died. Other events were like the ones we see in today's Olympics. During the fourth century B.C., the games were held at Olympia. ③

Ancient Greek pottery shows one of the first Olympic events, a chariot race.

Stop and Think

③ How might the Olympics have begun?

The Olympics might have begun when _____

_____

_____

Emperor Nero ruled the Roman Empire for fourteen years in the first century.

The ancient Greek games may have been dangerous, but everyone still followed Greek ideals and ethics. Sportsmanship and fairness were valued, and the emphasis was on physical skills.

That all changed when the Romans took over Greece. Then the games were regarded as entertainment. According to one account, the Roman emperor Nero competed in an Olympics. Nero wasn't a good athlete, but everyone was afraid of him. They let him win every event he entered. In the chariot race, he even fell out of his chariot! The other racers stopped right away to give Nero plenty of time to get back into the race. Of course, Nero won the wreath.

In A.D. 393, the games were stopped, and it seemed as if the Olympics had ended for good. ❹

Ancient Roman art shows a four-horse chariot race.

Stop and Think

❹ Do you think the chariot race was fair? Explain your answer.

I think that the chariot race _____

_____

_____

© Harcourt

But the Olympic spirit didn't die. In 1896, the modern games began once again in Greece. Influenced by the ancient Greek philosophy of fairness for all people, the founders of the modern Olympics had a dream. They believed the games could unite the citizens of different lands. By opening the contest to all athletes, no matter where they lived, they hoped to promote peace. **5**

Olympic athletes compete in the 1896 games in Greece.

Stop and Think

5 Do you think the founders' dream will come true? Explain your answer.

I think that the founders' dream _____

_____

_____

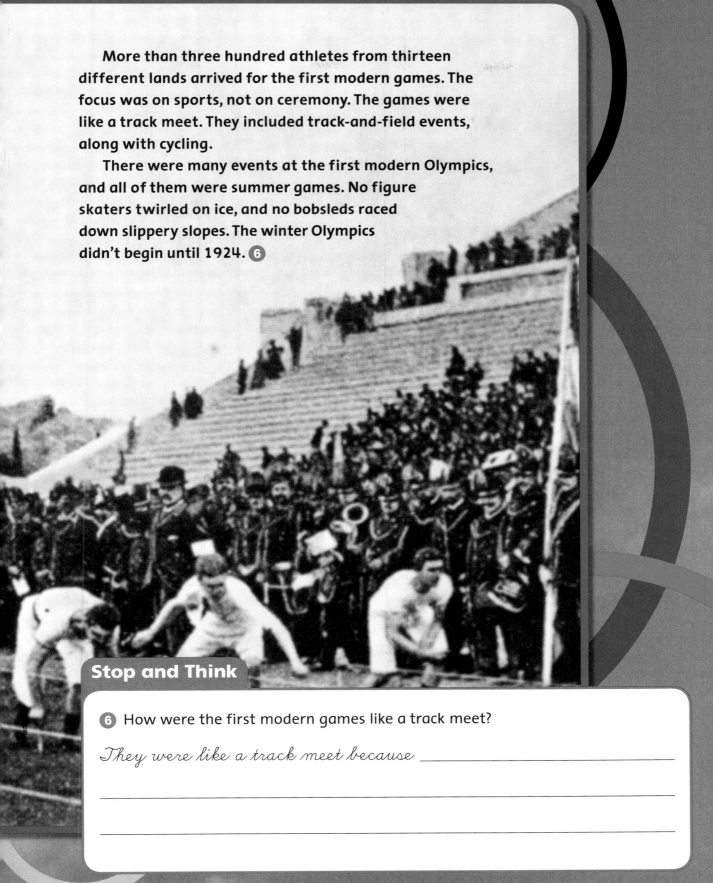

More than three hundred athletes from thirteen different lands arrived for the first modern games. The focus was on sports, not on ceremony. The games were like a track meet. They included track-and-field events, along with cycling.

There were many events at the first modern Olympics, and all of them were summer games. No figure skaters twirled on ice, and no bobsleds raced down slippery slopes. The winter Olympics didn't begin until 1924. **6**

Stop and Think

6 How were the first modern games like a track meet?

They were like a track meet because _____

_____

_____

Today, the winter and summer Olympics are major events that are celebrated across the world. Every two years, the best athletes gather in pursuit of medals for hundreds of events. In the 2004 Olympics, athletes came from more than two hundred different countries.

The Greeks who competed in the first Olympics would be surprised by what the games have become today. They would be astonished by the crowds. They would also be surprised to see female athletes, and they might wonder what happened to their leafy crowns. But they would be happy to know that the games still uphold the ideals and values of ancient Greece. **7**

Stop and Think

7 Why might the ancient Greeks not like seeing female athletes?

They might not like seeing female athletes because _____

_____

_____

Think Critically

1. How do the modern Olympics promote ancient Greek values? **MAIN IDEA AND DETAILS**

The modern Olympics promote ancient Greek values

by _____

_____

_____

2. How are today's Olympic games similar to the ancient Olympic games? Fill in the Venn diagram. **COMPARE AND CONTRAST**

Ancient Olympics | **Both** | **Today's Olympics**

no women

win wreaths

only Greek athletes

men and women

win medals

athletes from around the world

3. Why does the author compare the ancient Olympics to the modern Olympics? **AUTHOR'S PURPOSE**

The author compares the two events because _____

_____

_____

lustrous

precede

prolong

resigned

restored

strategically

temperaments

trespass

Vocabulary

Build Robust Vocabulary

Write the Vocabulary Word that completes each sentence. The first one has been done for you.

In 1940, four French teenagers discovered cave paintings made around twenty thousand years ago in Lascaux, France. The paintings give us insight into the moods and **(1)** _____temperaments_____ of the artists who created them. They show that the cave dwellers who lived thousands of years ago were not **(2)** _____ to a life of just trying to stay alive. They were skilled artists who knew how to show depth in their art. Sometimes, they **(3)** _____ placed bison on a curving wall to make them appear more lifelike.

The cave paintings found in 1940 aren't the only examples we have of prehistoric art. In 1994, three explorers found much older cave paintings in a different part of France. These paintings **(4)** _____ the Lascaux paintings by ten thousand years. This means that thirty thousand years ago, artists were making paintings of their world.

Over time, exposing the Lascaux cave paintings to the carbon dioxide in visitors' breath made the art less **(5)** _____ . To prevent further fading of the Lascaux art, the caves were closed to the public in 1963. The cave paintings have since been cleaned and **(6)** _____ to their original state.

The cave paintings that were found in 1994 were closed to the public right away. The reason for this was to **(7)** _____ the life of the art. The air in this cave is strictly regulated to protect the paintings. An alarm system stops anyone who might try to **(8)** _____ and go where they should not.

Write the Vocabulary Word that best completes the synonym web.

9.

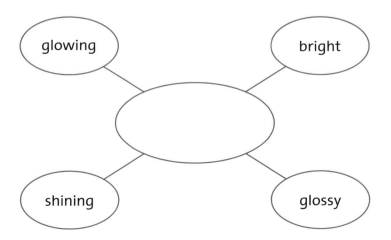

glowing

bright

shining

glossy

The Caves
Where Art Was Born

by David Neufeld

On Thursday, September 12, 1940, four French teenagers crawled into a cave near Lascaux, France, and discovered where artists had been at work thousands of years before. As the boys entered the cave, light from their oil lamp cast strange shadows on the walls. What they saw took their breath away. Animals from the late Ice Age were spread across the stone above their heads. Running bison, horses, and reindeer had been painted in lustrous shades of reds, browns, and yellows.

The teenagers' discovery has changed the way we think about Stone Age cave dwellers. We no longer believe that the dwellers were resigned to a life of just trying to stay alive. On the contrary, these amazing cave paintings have given us ready insights into their temperaments, interests, and artistic skills. **1**

Stop and Think

1 What do you think you will learn from this selection?

I think I will learn _____

_____

_____

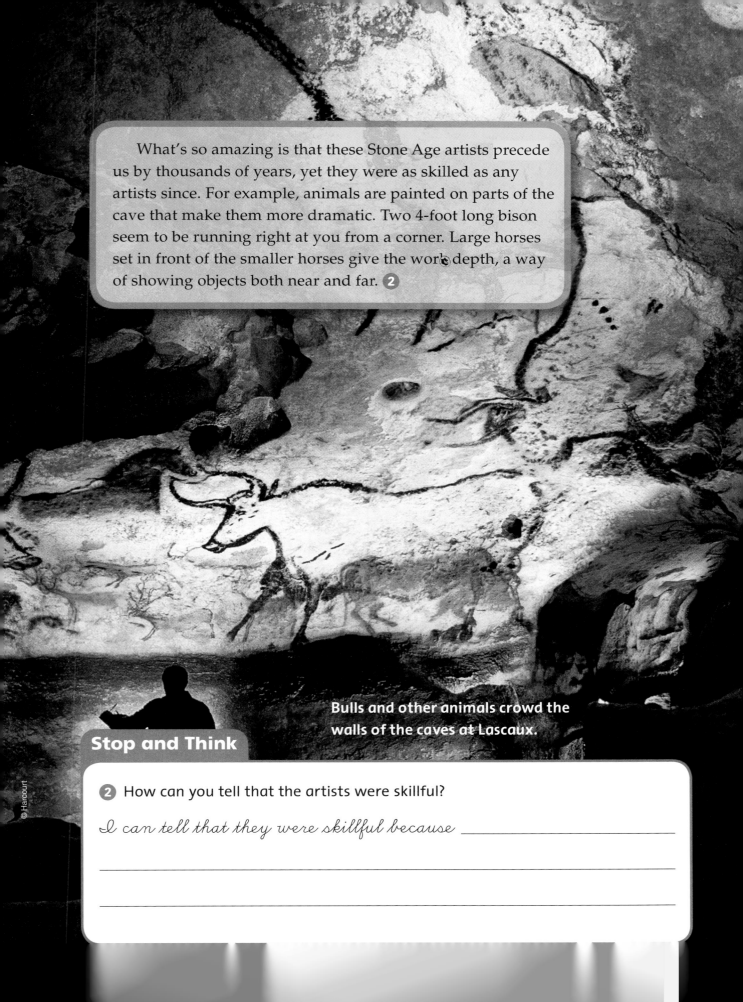

What's so amazing is that these Stone Age artists precede us by thousands of years, yet they were as skilled as any artists since. For example, animals are painted on parts of the cave that make them more dramatic. Two 4-foot long bison seem to be running right at you from a corner. Large horses set in front of the smaller horses give the work depth, a way of showing objects both near and far. **2**

Bulls and other animals crowd the walls of the caves at Lascaux.

Stop and Think

2 How can you tell that the artists were skillful?

I can tell that they were skillful because _____

_____

_____

The animals in front are darker than the ones behind them.

At one time, the use of depth in art was believed to be invented only hundreds of years ago. It's now clear that artists had already found a way to create depth on cave walls more than seventeen thousand years ago.

Here are three tricks that Stone Age artists used on two bison in the caves at Lascaux.

- They set one animal in front of another. Where the animals' bodies overlapped, they made the front animal darker in color or left a light line between them.
- When an animal's leg was on the far side of its body, they left a little space between the leg and the body to show some of the background.
- The artists made the front of the bison larger than the rear, something we expect to see when an animal is coming at us. And, they strategically placed the bison on a curving wall.

Pretty clever for artists who lived thousands of years ago, wouldn't you say? ③

Why does the author explain three tricks used by Stone Age artists?

The author explains the three tricks because _____

_____

_____

© Harcourt

Many of the cave paintings are out of reach for any painter of normal height. Experts believe that Stone Age artists used wood poles tied together to make a platform for working. Holes found in some of the upper parts of the cave walls confirm this.

These artists mixed their own paints by grinding up stones into colorful powders, then mixing them with water. They applied the paint using brushes made from animal hair or crushed sticks. Some experts think that the artists even used hollow bone or reed tubes to blow paint onto the cave walls.

How could these artists create masterpieces in such dark caves? It's believed that they used fat-burning lamps and wood torches to light the caves. It must have been smoky, smelly, sweaty work. **4**

The artists used different colors, such as red, yellow, brown, and black.

Stop and Think

4 What do you learn about tools used by Stone Age artists?

I learn that _____

_____

_____

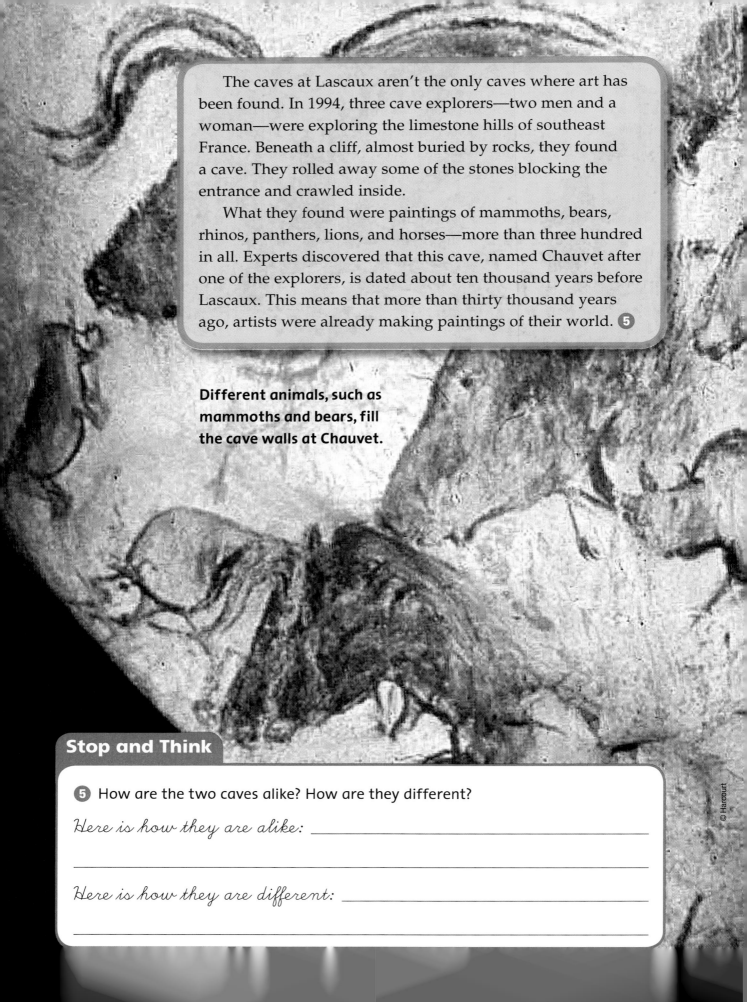

The caves at Lascaux aren't the only caves where art has been found. In 1994, three cave explorers—two men and a woman—were exploring the limestone hills of southeast France. Beneath a cliff, almost buried by rocks, they found a cave. They rolled away some of the stones blocking the entrance and crawled inside.

What they found were paintings of mammoths, bears, rhinos, panthers, lions, and horses—more than three hundred in all. Experts discovered that this cave, named Chauvet after one of the explorers, is dated about ten thousand years before Lascaux. This means that more than thirty thousand years ago, artists were already making paintings of their world. **5**

Different animals, such as mammoths and bears, fill the cave walls at Chauvet.

Stop and Think

5 How are the two caves alike? How are they different?

Here is how they are alike: _____

_____

Here is how they are different: _____

_____

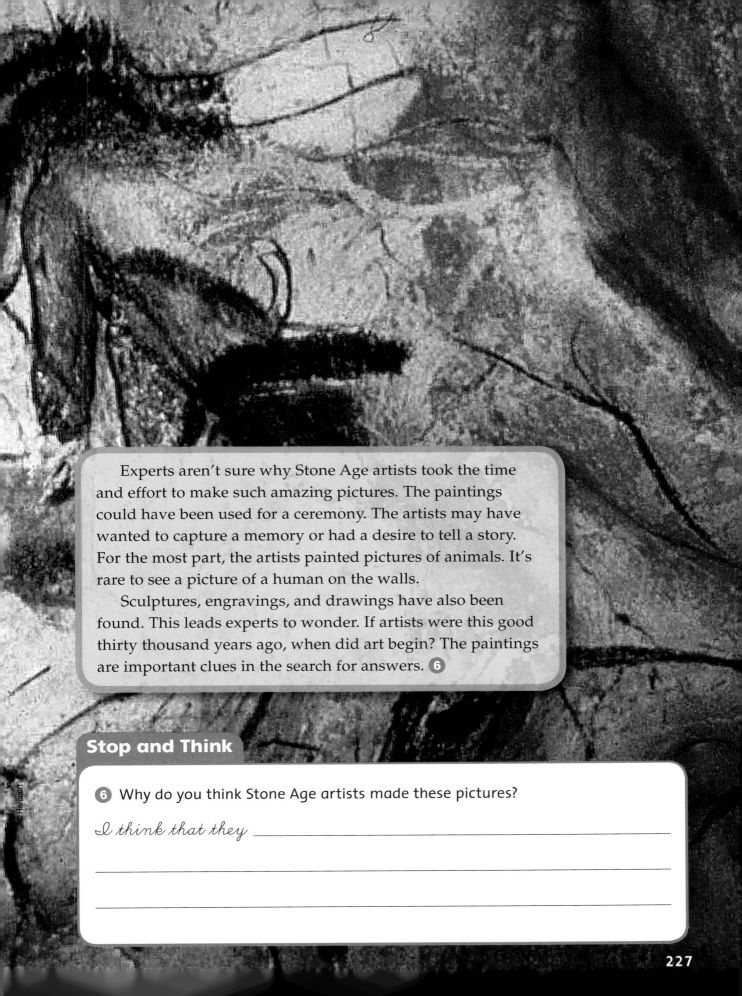

Experts aren't sure why Stone Age artists took the time and effort to make such amazing pictures. The paintings could have been used for a ceremony. The artists may have wanted to capture a memory or had a desire to tell a story. For the most part, the artists painted pictures of animals. It's rare to see a picture of a human on the walls.

Sculptures, engravings, and drawings have also been found. This leads experts to wonder. If artists were this good thirty thousand years ago, when did art begin? The paintings are important clues in the search for answers. **6**

Stop and Think

6 Why do you think Stone Age artists made these pictures?

I think that they _____

_____

_____

It's a good thing the artists chose to paint in caves, or these clues would no longer exist. The caves helped to prolong the life of the paintings by protecting them from the weather. If exposed to rain and wind, the paintings would have been long gone.

The only threat to the art is in the air inside the caves. Once the Lascaux paintings were discovered, visitors flocked to see the ancient art. Carbon dioxide in their breath caused the paintings to begin to fade. In 1963, the Lascaux caves were closed to the public and the paintings were restored to their original state. The Chauvet cave was protected from this threat right away, and since then, experts have made sure that the air inside is regulated with strict measures. They have also made sure no one can trespass on this important site.

Now, the cave paintings are guarded like buried treasure. These treasures can help us learn more about the people who may have been the world's first artists. **7**

Carbon dioxide caused the paintings to corrode, or rust.

Stop and Think

7 Why were the Lascaux caves closed to the public?

They were closed to the public because _____

_____

_____

Think Critically

1. What have you learned about Stone Age artists? **MAIN IDEA AND DETAILS**

I have learned that Stone Age artists _____

_____

_____

2. What did the Stone Age artists have in common with today's artists? Fill in the Venn diagram. **COMPARE AND CONTRAST**

Stone Age Artists   **Both**   **Today's Artists**

lived long ago

made own paints and supplies

live in the present

buy paints and supplies

3. Why does the author compare the paintings to "buried treasure"? **AUTHOR'S PURPOSE**

The author compares them to "buried treasure" because

_____

_____

_____

befitting

disposition

dispute

revered

savory

tolerated

unsettling

vigilantly

Vocabulary

Build Robust Vocabulary

Read the story and think about the meanings of the words in dark type.

Inti [IN•tee] and his eight children lived long ago, high in the Andes Mountains. They were a most **revered** family. Many respected them for their great knowledge and skills.

Inti's children were very talented. One knew how to cook **savory** dishes. Another was a master at making strong shelters made of stone. Each had mastered a skill, except Inti's two youngest children, Manco [MAN•koh] and Mamak [MAH•mak]. But like the older children, they always behaved in a manner **befitting** the children of Inti.

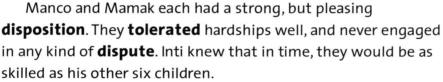

Manco and Mamak each had a strong, but pleasing **disposition**. They **tolerated** hardships well, and never engaged in any kind of **dispute**. Inti knew that in time, they would be as skilled as his other six children.

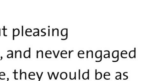

Inti was very wise. He saw that the world beyond their lake home was wild and had no order. Humans roamed the earth like animals. They had no skills and could not care for themselves. Inti got an **unsettling** feeling each time he began to think about it. He **vigilantly** searched for a way to fix the problem. Then one day, he realized that he could get his talented children to help.

© Harcourt

**Write the answers to these questions. Use complete sentences.
The first one has been done for you.**

1. Inti's family was **revered**. What does this mean?

   It means that his family was respected and admired by others.

   _____

2. What is a **savory** dish?

   _____

   _____

3. What does it mean to "behave in a manner **befitting** the children
   of Inti"?

   _____

   _____

4. What is the **disposition** of someone who **tolerates** hardships well?

   _____

   _____

5. What is a **dispute**?

   _____

   _____

6. What is an **unsettling** feeling? What can make you feel that way?

   _____

   _____

7. What might a person do if they were **vigilantly** searching for the
   answer to a problem?

   _____

   _____

The Eight Children of Inti

retold by Cheryl Allison

illustrated by Bee Willey

Long ago, Inti [IN•tee] and his eight children lived on a lake high in the Andes Mountains. They were a most revered family. Many respected them for their great knowledge and skills.

Inti possessed great wisdom and saw that the world beyond the lake was wild and had no order. Humans roamed the earth like animals and possessed no skills to care for themselves or others. Inti wanted to help them learn survival skills, so they would not go hungry and suffer. **1**

Stop and Think

1 Why is Inti's family so revered?

Inti's family is so revered because _____

_____

_____

This problem weighed on Inti's mind. Then he realized that his children could help. His son, Uchu [EW•choo], was a great farmer. He could teach others how to grow crops. This would keep them from going hungry.

His son, Cachi [KAH•chee], was a master at creating strong shelters of stone. He could teach those beyond the lake how to use stones to construct homes that would keep them warm and dry.

Inti's son Auca [ah•EW•kah] was a great toolmaker. He could teach others how to make tools that would help them farm the land and make their homes. **2**

Stop and Think

2 What can Inti's sons teach the people beyond the lake?

Inti's sons can teach the people _____

_____

_____

Inti's daughter Cora [KOR•ah] knew how to make savory dishes and could teach those beyond the lake to cook. She could also instruct them on how to save and store their food.

Inti's daughter Raura [rah•OR•ah] could teach others how to spin and weave wool. Warm clothes would protect them from the cold.

Inti's daughter Huaco [ew•AH•koh] could instruct those beyond the lake on how to turn clay into cups and bowls. Jars could be made for storing seed and grain.

The two youngest of Inti's eight children were Manco [MAN•koh] and Mamak [MAH•mak]. They were not as skilled as their brothers and sisters, but their strong disposition made them fast learners. **3**

Stop and Think

3 How are Inti's two youngest children different from their brothers and sisters?

Inti's two youngest children _____

_____

_____

Inti summoned his eight children and placed his challenge before them. "I have a great task for you," he said. "You must leave your home and travel far, teaching your skills to all you meet. Then you must establish a great city in which you, and your children after you, will reign."

As he explained his plan, Inti displayed a golden rod and handed it to his oldest child. "You must find land that is rich enough to grow and sustain corn and other crops," he told his children. "When you reach a place where the ground breaks under the weight of this rod on the first blow, then you will be in the right place to establish a great city." **4**

Stop and Think

4 How might the rod be a symbol?

The rod might be a symbol of _____

_____

_____

Before the eight children departed, their father added, "If a dispute should arise among you, don't get angry and let it prevent you from completing your task. Always behave in a manner befitting the children of Inti."

Sometimes they stopped for a few months or years at a time to teach their skills to everybody they met. They tested the ground in many new places to see if it would break under the weight of the rod, but they failed each time. Their repeated failure to break the ground with the rod was unsettling. Cachi began to complain that this task was not possible. Uchu and Auca started to grumble, too. **5**

Stop and Think

5 What do you think will happen next?

I think that _____

_____

_____

© Harcourt

Then Raura and Cora began to say that their feet were wearing out. Huaco the potter said that she, too, couldn't take another step.

The only two of the eight children who didn't complain were the youngest ones, Manco and Mamak. Because of their strong wills, they tolerated hardship well.

Finally, Manco and Mamak decided that they must continue to lead the journey. The young leaders searched vigilantly for 180 years longer, until they reached a summit high in the Andes Mountains, overlooking a great valley. With all his strength, Manco threw down the rod. Everyone breathed a great sigh of relief when the golden rod sank into the ground. This valley is where they founded the great city of Cusco and established the Inca as supreme rulers. ❻

Stop and Think

❻ How can you tell that this is a legend?

I can tell that this is a legend because _____

_____

_____

During their years of travel, Manco and Mamak had learned many important skills by watching their brothers and sisters. Manco became a master farmer, architect, and toolmaker. He taught the members of the Inca Empire to grow crops and to make strong, stone structures.

Mamak became a master cook, clothmaker, and potter. She instructed the members of the Inca Empire on how to cook, spin, weave, and make pottery.

Today, the Andes is known for the beautiful cloth and pottery crafted there. It's also known for the farming terraces and for the well-constructed stone shelters that still stand. **7**

Stop and Think

7 According to the legend, why is the Andes known for its cloth and pottery?

It's known for cloth and pottery because _____

_____

_____

© Harcourt

Think Critically

1. What is the turning point in this legend? **PLOT**

   The turning point is when _____

   _____

   _____

2. What traits helped Manco and Mamak finish their difficult task? Write your answers in the web. **CHARACTERS**

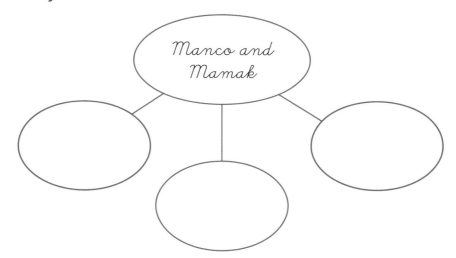

   Manco and Mamak

3. What does this legend try to explain? **AUTHOR'S PURPOSE**

   This legend tries to explain _____

   _____

   _____

descendants	
fertile	
flourishing	
immortalized	
intact	
primitive	
reinforces	
rituals	

Vocabulary

Build Robust Vocabulary

Write the Vocabulary Word that completes each sentence in the selection. The first one has been done for you.

Inside the Ruins

by Mary J. Martin

An amazing sight was spread out before my eyes. Stone walls had been fitted together like a giant puzzle, high on a mountain ridge. I was looking at what was left of the Inca city of Machu Picchu [MAH•choo PEE•choo]. Hundreds of years ago, this city was part of a **(1)** _____flourishing_____ empire that grew until it stretched across what is now Peru. Stone-paved roads still wind through the green, **(2)** _____ jungles where many crops grow. The paths lead up the rocky mountain to Machu Picchu.

Today, much of the city of Machu Picchu still stands **(3)** _____.

One can walk the streets and see buildings made of the huge stone blocks. Though they are long gone, the Inca are **(4)** _____ for all time in these lasting structures.

240

Each stone wall **(5)** _____
the belief that the Inca were skilled experts at
building things. The Inca cut huge stones into
different shapes and fitted them together perfectly
to make homes and other structures. Some structures may have
been used for **(6)** _____ , or ceremonies.

Amazingly, some of the stones weigh as much as 50
tons. Somehow, the Inca carried these heavy stones up
the steep mountain ridge and placed them where they still
stand today. Many experts wonder if the Inca had some
(7) _____ devices, such as ropes or
wedges, to help them. No one really knows how they did this.
Not even the **(8)** _____ of the Inca know
how the structures were made.

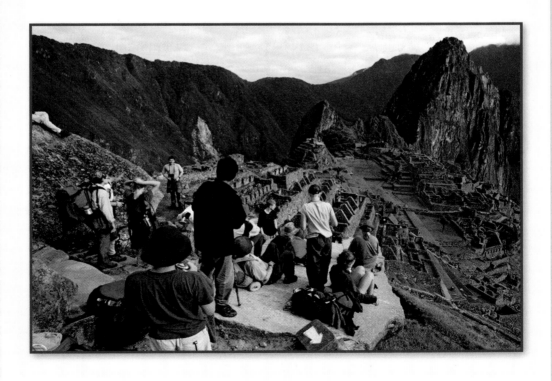

Stone Puzzle

by David Neufeld

illustrated by Paul Zwolak

Hundreds of years ago in what is now Peru, the Inca lived in the center of a flourishing empire. This center was Machu Picchu (MAH•choo PEE•choo), a stone city built on a high mountain ridge. Machu Picchu is the only Inca city that is still intact. Rediscovered by a professor from Yale University in 1911, it is one of the eight wonders of the world.

Many people wonder how huge cut stones were fitted together to make walls, homes, and other places in this mountaintop city. The stones, some measuring as wide as 10 feet and weighing more than 50 tons, must have somehow been brought up the steep sides of the mountain to the site. This may be possible today, but hundreds of years ago it was a real feat. **1**

Stop and Think

1 Why was building Machu Picchu a "real feat"?

It was a "real feat" because _____

_____

_____

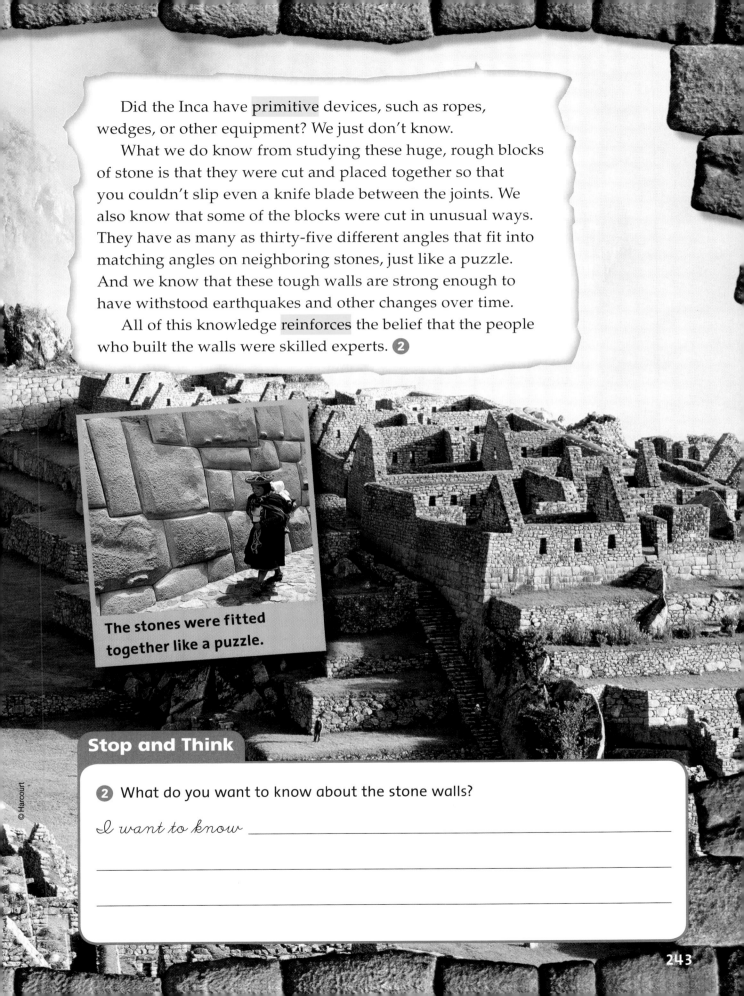

Did the Inca have primitive devices, such as ropes, wedges, or other equipment? We just don't know.

What we do know from studying these huge, rough blocks of stone is that they were cut and placed together so that you couldn't slip even a knife blade between the joints. We also know that some of the blocks were cut in unusual ways. They have as many as thirty-five different angles that fit into matching angles on neighboring stones, just like a puzzle. And we know that these tough walls are strong enough to have withstood earthquakes and other changes over time.

All of this knowledge reinforces the belief that the people who built the walls were skilled experts. ❷

The stones were fitted together like a puzzle.

Stop and Think

❷ What do you want to know about the stone walls?

I want to know _____

_____

_____

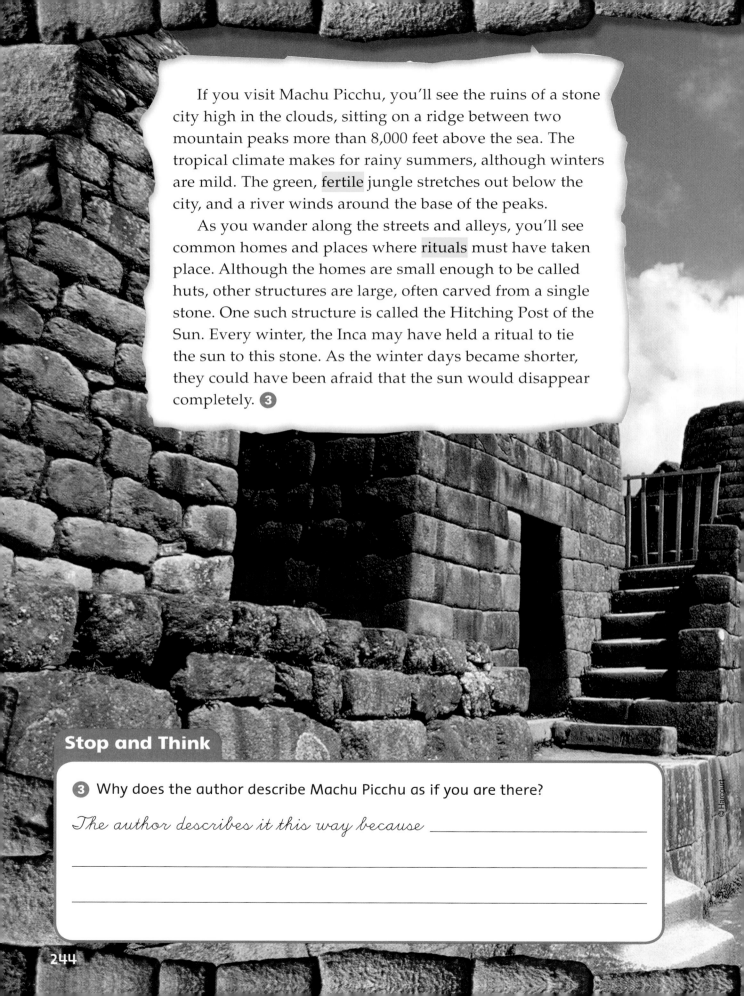

If you visit Machu Picchu, you'll see the ruins of a stone city high in the clouds, sitting on a ridge between two mountain peaks more than 8,000 feet above the sea. The tropical climate makes for rainy summers, although winters are mild. The green, fertile jungle stretches out below the city, and a river winds around the base of the peaks.

As you wander along the streets and alleys, you'll see common homes and places where rituals must have taken place. Although the homes are small enough to be called huts, other structures are large, often carved from a single stone. One such structure is called the Hitching Post of the Sun. Every winter, the Inca may have held a ritual to tie the sun to this stone. As the winter days became shorter, they could have been afraid that the sun would disappear completely. ❸

Stop and Think

❸ Why does the author describe Machu Picchu as if you are there?

The author describes it this way because _____

_____

_____

244

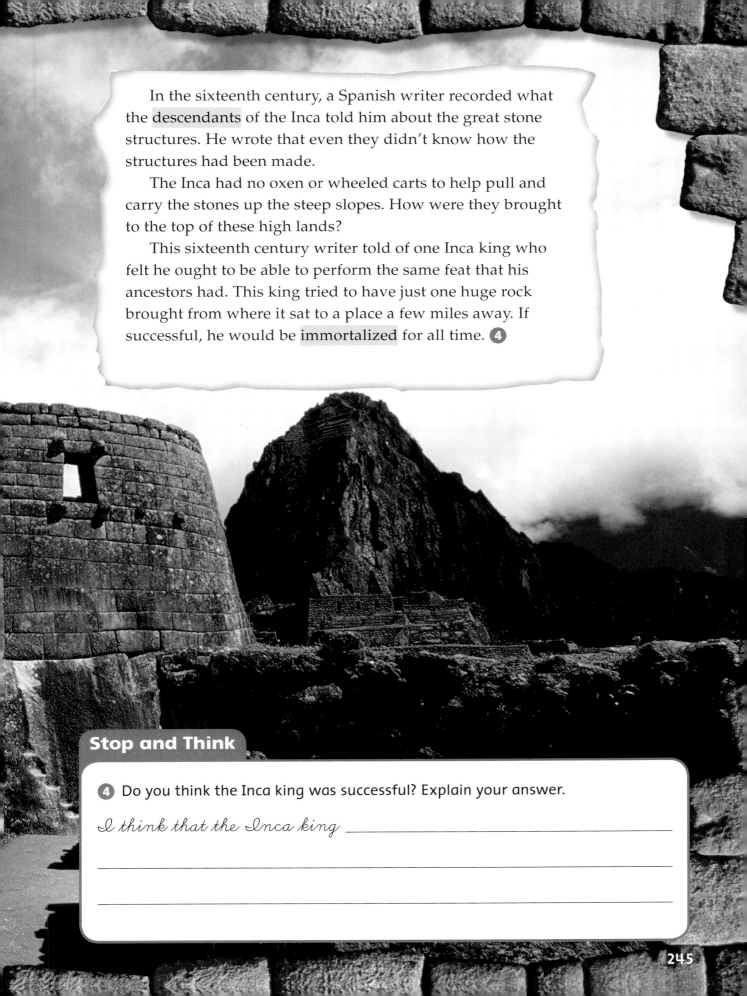

In the sixteenth century, a Spanish writer recorded what the descendants of the Inca told him about the great stone structures. He wrote that even they didn't know how the structures had been made.

The Inca had no oxen or wheeled carts to help pull and carry the stones up the steep slopes. How were they brought to the top of these high lands?

This sixteenth century writer told of one Inca king who felt he ought to be able to perform the same feat that his ancestors had. This king tried to have just one huge rock brought from where it sat to a place a few miles away. If successful, he would be immortalized for all time. **4**

Stop and Think

4 Do you think the Inca king was successful? Explain your answer.

I think that the Inca king _____

_____

_____

The writer said that more than twenty thousand workers tried to haul the big rock across the rough land. At one point, the rock fell from the workers' hands and crushed more than three thousand people. The stone then rolled off a cliff, putting an end to the king's foolish attempt.

The king's effort showed what a complex task it must have been to carve huge rocks into jigsaw puzzle pieces, lift them, and fit them together. Even today we can't call it primitive work. ⑤

Stop and Think

⑤ Why can't we call the Inca's work primitive?

We can't call it primitive because _____

_____

_____

©Harcourt

However, the stone structures are not the only puzzles to be uncovered in Machu Picchu. At one time, as many as three hundred Inca may have lived in the city, and many fountains and other structures throughout the city held water for drinking and bathing. How did they get so much water on this high mountaintop?

Kenneth Wright studied this puzzle for six years. He and his team found a water spring used by the Inca on a higher mountain slope. This spring collected and held rainwater from the frequent tropical rains. The team discovered that the Inca made the spring bigger by building stone walls to hold back the water. Then they made a stone trench to carry the water to the city's sixteen fountains. Wright said that the Inca must have put much thought into planning this complex water system. **6**

The fountain stones were placed so they would create a water spout.

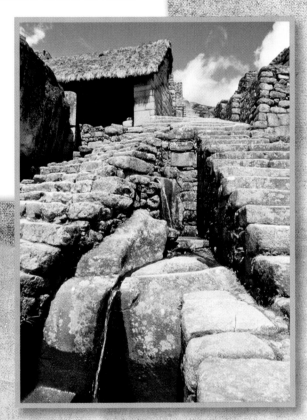

Stop and Think

6 How did the Inca supply their city with water?

The Inca _____

_____

_____

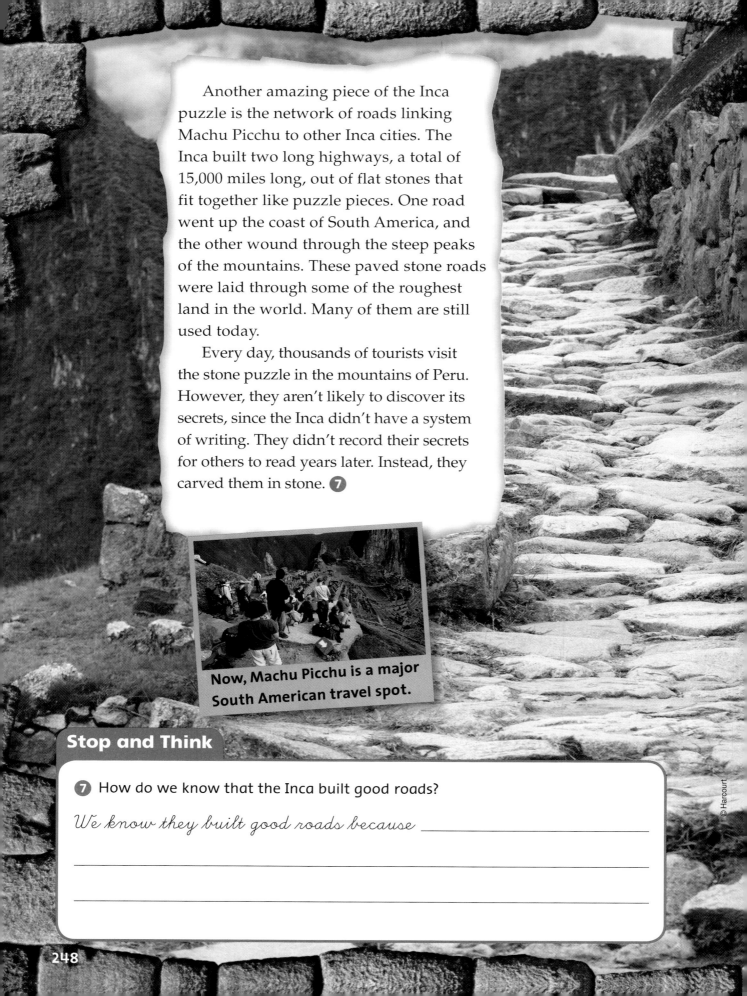

Another amazing piece of the Inca puzzle is the network of roads linking Machu Picchu to other Inca cities. The Inca built two long highways, a total of 15,000 miles long, out of flat stones that fit together like puzzle pieces. One road went up the coast of South America, and the other wound through the steep peaks of the mountains. These paved stone roads were laid through some of the roughest land in the world. Many of them are still used today.

Every day, thousands of tourists visit the stone puzzle in the mountains of Peru. However, they aren't likely to discover its secrets, since the Inca didn't have a system of writing. They didn't record their secrets for others to read years later. Instead, they carved them in stone. **7**

Now, Machu Picchu is a major South American travel spot.

Stop and Think

7 How do we know that the Inca built good roads?

We know they built good roads because _____

_____

_____

©Harcourt

Think Critically

1. What have you learned about Machu Picchu? Complete the third column of the K-W-L chart. **MAIN IDEA AND DETAILS**

What I Know	What I Want To Know	What I Learned

2. Why was Machu Picchu so difficult to build? **CAUSE AND EFFECT**

   Machu Picchu was so difficult to build because _____

   _____

   _____

3. What two meanings could the title "Stone Puzzle" have?
   AUTHOR'S CRAFT

   The title "Stone Puzzle" could mean _____

   _____

   _____

Vocabulary

Build Robust Vocabulary

Write the word that best completes each sentence.
The first one has been done for you.

1. Uncle Ted and the kids will be impressed when they see the

_____**imposing**_____ stone circles of Europe.

pillaged   aggravated   imposing

2. The ones in Ireland, Scotland, and England are famous. They

are the most _____ stone circles

ornery   notable   unassuming

in the world.

3. After a long flight from Boston, the kids get

_____. They complain about

unassuming   ornery   sophisticated

being hungry and tired.

4. Uncle Ted tries not to be _____ by

aggravated   prosperous   conspicuous

their complaints.

5. The next day, they go to Newgrange. They see a gift

shop, guards, and lots of tourists there. It must

be a _____

ornery   unassuming   prosperous

tourist attraction.

6. Newgrange is not as grand as the pyramids. It's more

_____ , but it's still very interesting.

unassuming   sophisticated   conspicuous

7. The people who created Newgrange had an

advanced and complex culture. Their culture was

_____ .

conspicuous   sophisticated   aggravated

8. Like the pyramids, the Newgrange tomb has been

_____ by thieves over time.

aggravated   pillaged   reinforced

9. "This is so _____ !" Lily says. She

ornery   prosperous   overwhelming

doesn't know how to take it all in.

10. Next they will go to Callanish in Scotland. The stones there

are _____ on a high hill,

conspicuous   unassuming   prosperous

and can be seen from far away.

VISITING THE STONE CIRCLES

by David Neufeld

CHARACTERS

NARRATOR   UNCLE TED
LILY   ROCKY
AIRPORT ATTENDANT   TOURIST CHORUS

NARRATOR: Ted Copeland is taking his niece and nephew to Europe to see the famous stone circles. Circles made of stone pillars are found throughout the world, and some of them are thousands of years old. The most notable ones are in Ireland, Scotland, and England. The three travelers begin their trip at Boston's Logan Airport.

UNCLE TED: Get out your passports, kids.

LILY: I've got mine. I was having a bad hair day when they took this picture!

AIRPORT ATTENDANT: Have any of these bags been out of your sight since you packed them?

ROCKY: Ummm, I didn't pack mine; my mom did.

AIRPORT ATTENDANT: Just place your suitcases on the table there, and we'll have a look. ❶

Stop and Think

❶ What do you learn about stone circles?

I learn that stone circles _____

_____

_____

NARRATOR: Just seven hours after they fasten their seatbelts, they arrive in Dublin, Ireland. Soon they're on their way by car through the green hills of Ireland.

ROCKY: I'm so tired my brain feels numb. When are we going to stop for a nap?

LILY: I'm starving, too, Uncle Ted—all I've had to eat since last night is airplane food. Are we there yet?

UNCLE TED: Now, kids, don't get ornery on me. We're almost to the inn so try not to complain . . . unless you want an aggravated uncle on your hands! We'll get a hot meal and some rest soon. **2**

Stop and Think

2 How do you think Uncle Ted feels?

I think Uncle Ted feels _____

_____

_____

NARRATOR: The next morning just before sunrise, the three tourists arrive at the stone circle of Newgrange. A huge, imposing stone carved with spirals sits at the entrance to the tomb.

UNCLE TED: This stone circle is about five thousand years old and was created around an earth mound.

TOURIST CHORUS: Wow! Look at the huge stones!

ROCKY: Didn't they use Newgrange as a burial place, like the pyramids?

LILY: Sorry, Rocky, you won't find mummies here.

UNCLE TED: Yes, Newgrange is a passage tomb, Rocky. A passage tomb is a burial chamber that can only be reached by walking through a long passage. While it's more unassuming than the pyramids, experts believe Newgrange was created *before* the pyramids.

NARRATOR: The sun's first rays bathe Newgrange in an orange glow. A moment later, the stone at the end of the passage tomb glistens in the morning light. **3**

Newgrange

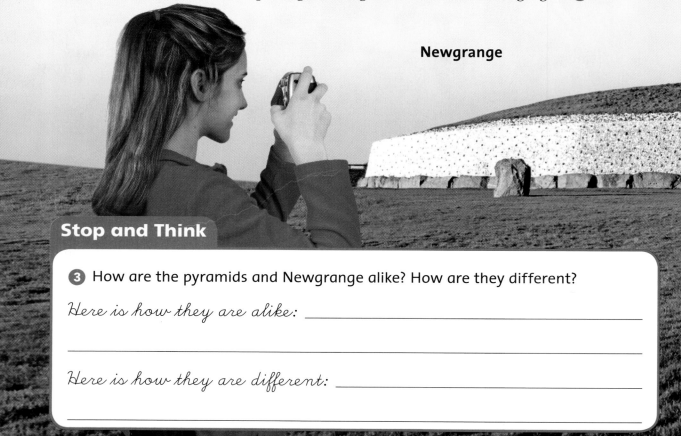

Stop and Think

3 How are the pyramids and Newgrange alike? How are they different?

Here is how they are alike: _____

_____

Here is how they are different: _____

_____

UNCLE TED: Every winter, a beam of light from the rising sun shines into the chamber. Experts say that the entrance to the passage tomb faces east to capture the rays of the rising sun. A lot of stone circles seem to be arranged so people can gaze at the sky. This may have been a way for them to keep track of time, sort of like a stone calendar.

LILY: This is so overwhelming! I can't believe this was made thousands of years ago!

ROCKY: It says in this booklet that the people who created Newgrange had a sophisticated culture. There's evidence that they farmed the land and owned animals such as cattle and pigs.

UNCLE TED: These places, like the pyramids, have been pillaged by thieves over time. One time, a man even tried to pry the spiral stones loose but failed. ❹

First light at Newgrange

Stop and Think

❹ What do you think they will do next?

I think they will _____

_____

_____

NARRATOR: Four days later, Uncle Ted, Lily, and Rocky are standing in front of Callanish, a stone circle in Scotland. The stones are conspicuous on a high, bleak hill, and can be seen from far away.

UNCLE TED: Callanish is called the "place of sadness" because of its solemn appearance. From a distance, the thirteen stone columns look like a line of human beings.

NARRATOR: Lily shivers and hunches over, clutching the front of her jacket together. She peers at the strange stone shapes on the top of the hillside.

LILY: I can feel the sadness of this place.

ROCKY: It certainly doesn't look as prosperous as Newgrange. There's no gift shop, no guards, and not very many tourists. ⑤

Callanish

Stop and Think

⑤ How are the stone columns like a line of humans?

The stone columns _____

_____

_____

NARRATOR: Two days later, the travelers are in England, standing dumbstruck in front of the most visited stone circle in the world—Stonehenge.

LILY: I liked Callanish better, even though it was so quiet and plain. Callanish didn't have a chain-link fence around it.

UNCLE TED: We mustn't forget that they had to put a fence around Stonehenge. There were too many visitors, and they didn't want this important site pillaged or damaged.

LILY: How did people get those gigantic stones here?

ROCKY: No one really knows. It says in this book that each of those imposing stones weighs an overwhelming 50 tons.

TOURIST CHORUS: Wow—50 tons? That's the weight of a humpback whale! ❻

Stop and Think

❻ Why is there a fence around Stonehenge?

There's a fence around Stonehenge because _____

_____

_____

NARRATOR: A crowd of tourists swarms around the site, pressing their faces against the chain-link fence.

TOURIST CHORUS: Can't we get any closer?

LILY: Will we ever know why stone circles were created, Uncle Ted?

UNCLE TED: I doubt it. There are so many possible reasons, such as to bury the dead, to worship, to star-gaze, and even just to gather the community together.

ROCKY: Newgrange seemed to be both a burying place *and* a star-gazing center.

UNCLE TED: Well, kids, we've seen some of the most notable stone circles in all of Great Britain. But did you know that there are nearly a thousand smaller circles to see?

LILY: Ummm, Uncle Ted, we won't have time to see all of them, will we? **7**

Stonehenge

Stop and Think

7 Why do you think people built stone circles?

I think people built stone circles because _____

_____

_____

Think Critically

1. How are all of the stone circles alike? How are they different?
COMPARE AND CONTRAST

Here is how they are alike: _____

_____

Here is how they are different: _____

_____

_____

2. What important fact have you learned about stone circles?
MAIN IDEA AND DETAILS

I have learned that _____

_____

_____

3. How do you think the author feels about protecting the stone circles? Explain your answer. AUTHOR'S VIEWPOINT

I think the author feels _____

_____

_____

barren

chasm

distinctive

impact

mottled

prominent

scale

warped

Vocabulary

Build Robust Vocabulary

Write the Vocabulary Word that completes each sentence in the newspaper articles. The first one has been done for you.

DAILY NEWS   SECTION C

Asteroid Seen at Star Party

by James Ramos

Monday, May 12

At a star party this past Saturday night, young astronomers pointed their telescopes to the skies. Mrs. Brown, a science teacher, assisted them. "One of my sixth grade students found an asteroid," reported Mrs. Brown. "She thought it was a comet. But it didn't have the **(1)** _____distinctive_____ tail that makes it possible to recognize a comet. That's how I knew that it was an asteroid."

Mrs. Brown explained that asteroids are like rocks. Some are **(2)** _____ with dark spots and other odd shapes and patterns. They also vary in size. Some of the more **(3)** _____ asteroids can even be 200 miles wide!

© Harcourt

Star Party Teaches About Space

by James Ramos

Monday, October 20

At the last star party in the park, Mrs. Brown's high-powered telescope had a **(4)** _____ lens that caused images to appear distorted. "Several children had smaller telescopes and were able to use them," said Mrs. Brown. "But the high-powered telescope allows us to see so much more."

Adjusting her plans for the party, Mrs. Brown talked to partygoers about the enormous **(5)** _____ of our universe. She also taught them about the asteroid that burst five miles above Earth's surface in 1908. "It didn't hit Earth, but the near **(6)** _____ burned up trees that were on the ground. It's lucky that the area was **(7)** _____ and unpopulated. If a city had been hit, the result could have been a major disaster." When a big meteorite slams into the earth, it creates an enormous hole, or **(8)** _____ , in the ground.

"I hope more people will join us for the next star party," Mrs. Brown said. "It's a great way to learn about the universe!"

The Asteroid Belt

by Susan Blackaby

On January 1, 1801, an astronomer named Piazzi aimed a telescope at the night sky. He spotted something unknown. At first he thought that it was a comet, but he soon had to rethink this idea. He knew that a comet follows a long path through space. It goes to the most remote rim of our solar system, and it has a distinctive tail. The tail can be seen only when the comet returns to pass close to the sun.

But the path of this new object was different. It was like the path of a small planet. Piazzi had discovered the first asteroid, a space object that orbits, or revolves around, the sun. **1**

Stop and Think

1 How is an asteroid like a small planet?

An asteroid is like a small planet because _____

_____

_____

What Are Asteroids?

Asteroids are like rocks. Some may be smooth, uneven blobs. Some may be mottled with both dark and light spots. Some may be solid chunks. They can be as small as pebbles, or they can be 200 feet wide. Some of the more prominent asteroids can even be 200 miles wide!

Scientists once thought asteroids were parts of an old planet that had exploded. Further study led them to reconsider this idea. For a start, not all asteroids are made of the same thing. This shows that they didn't all come from the same place. And even if all the asteroids were recombined to make one planet, it would be smaller than our own moon. So asteroids are likely what was left over when the planets formed. **2**

This asteroid is 35 miles wide.

Stop and Think

2 What did scientists learn from studying asteroids?

Scientists learned that _____

_____

_____

Telescopes Allow a Closer Look

Researching asteroids and other space objects would not be possible without telescopes. In the 1570s, Galileo made the first refracting telescope, a telescope that used shaped glass lenses to bend light rays. It allowed a close-up look at far-off objects. But the images were often distorted, or warped.

In the early 1600s, Johannes Kepler refined Galileo's model. Kepler's telescope was able to display a sharper image. However, the image was upside down.

In the late 1600s, Isaac Newton tried to rework Kepler's model. He decided to invent a new telescope instead. The result was a reflecting telescope that used mirrors as well as glass lenses. It gave a much clearer look.

At about the same time, a Frenchman named Cassegrain also made a reflecting telescope. Newton was not impressed and continued his own design. However, Cassegrain's basic telescope design is the one most used today. ❸

In Galileo's telescope, light entered the far end and passed through a glass lens, which bent the light rays. The person looking though the eyepiece could see a larger picture of the object.

Stop and Think

❸ Why does the author include facts about telescopes?

The author includes these facts because _____

_____

_____

This space probe was launched into space in 2004.

Researching Asteroids Today

As telescopes got stronger, more and more asteroids were discovered. By 1900, hundreds of asteroids had been discovered . Today, several hundred thousand asteroids have been recorded. Each year, thousands are added to the list.

Recent space probes have been able to study asteroids up close. They send images, as well as samples and data for maps, back to Earth for scientists to research. In 1999, one of these probes even landed on the surface of Eros, one of the larger asteroids that orbit the sun.

● ● ● ● ● ● ● ● ●

Most asteroids are labeled using only numbers, while some are named after characters in legends. The first asteroid was named Ceres, the Roman goddess of grain. Some honor heroes and other famous people, such as sports legend Jesse Owens and World War II writer Anne Frank.

4

Anne Frank

Stop and Think

4 What do you learn about space probes?

I learn that space probes _____

_____

_____

An Asteroid Superhighway

The Asteroid Belt is an area between Mars and Jupiter where the most asteroids are found. The asteroids in the belt follow a path shaped like a stretched-out circle. The scale of the solar system is large. It takes from three to six years for an asteroid to make one orbit around the sun.

The gravity on Jupiter, the largest planet, is what keeps the asteroids traveling along the same orbit. The gravity has kept the asteroids from regrouping to form a single body. And thanks to Jupiter's large mass, they don't disturb the rest of the planets closest to the sun, such as Mars, Mercury, Venus, and Earth.

Some asteroids are also moons, such as the smaller moons of Jupiter. In its early days as a planet, Jupiter may have pulled the asteroids into its orbit, where the asteroids became moons. In fact, Jupiter is like a small solar system, with at least sixty-one moons orbiting it. Many of these moons may be asteroids. **5**

Thousands of asteroids travel the main Asteroid Belt.

Stop and Think

5 How does Jupiter's large mass help the other planets?

Jupiter's large mass _____

_____

_____

Earth Grazers

Asteroids can be found outside the Asteroid Belt, too. Some cross paths with Earth as they move through space. These are called "Earth Grazers."

On June 30, 1908, a small asteroid burst five miles above Earth's surface in a part of Siberia called Tunguska. Trees burned up from the heat, and those that didn't burn were knocked flat. About 2,000 square miles were affected. It took a long time to repair the damage. It's lucky that the area was barren and unpopulated. If a city had been hit, the result could have been a major disaster.

On March 23, 1989, a fifty-million-ton asteroid passed by Earth. It was 400,000 miles from us when it passed by. That sounds like a safe distance, but Earth and the asteroid had missed each other by only about six hours. **6**

Stop and Think

6 What do you think you will learn about next?

I think I will learn _____

_____

_____

Meteors and Meteorites

When an asteroid enters our atmosphere, it's called a meteor. Most meteors burn up before they hit the ground. When you see a shooting star, you're really seeing a meteor burning up in our atmosphere. Meteors that land on Earth are called meteorites. When a large meteorite hits Earth, the impact can leave an enormous hole. One example of this is the Barringer Crater in Winslow, Arizona. The huge chasm was created about fifty thousand years ago when an asteroid about 150 feet wide slammed into Earth. It left a crater almost 4,000 feet wide and 650 feet deep. Thankfully, very large meteorites hit Earth only about once every million years.

People can find meteorites all over the world. You might even find one in your own backyard! Just look for a rock with a black crust. The crust may also include flaky brown or orange rust. A true meteorite will almost always attract a magnet, too. With luck, you can hold in your hands what's left of an asteroid that once floated in space. **7**

In 1920, the Barringer Crater in Arizona was identified as the first known crater caused by a meteorite.

© Harcourt

Stop and Think

7 What would you do if you found a meteorite?

I would _____

_____

_____

Think Critically

1. What new facts have you learned about asteroids? Complete the third column of the K-W-L chart. **MAIN IDEA AND DETAILS**

What I Know	What I Want to Know	What I Learned

2. What happens when asteroids enter our atmosphere? **CAUSE AND EFFECT**

When asteroids enter our atmosphere, _____

_____

_____

3. Why do scientists study asteroids? **DRAW CONCLUSIONS**

Scientists study asteroids because _____

_____

_____

_____

_____

ascent

doomed

dreaded

lavish

murky

remains

Vocabulary

Build Robust Vocabulary

Write the Vocabulary Word that completes each sentence. The first one has been done for you.

Mel Fisher is exploring for sunken treasure. He peers into the cloudy, **(1)** _____murky_____ water. Will this be the day he finds what has so far eluded him? Will he at last find what's left of the *Atocha,* the Spanish ship that sunk in 1622? Or will this be just another day of disappointment?

Fisher had been hunting for the **(2)** _____ of the *Atocha* for years. In 1963, he and his crew found part of the treasure. They found 1,033 gold coins on the sea floor. Fisher knew much more was still at the bottom of the sea somewhere. The ship was rumored to have carried **(3)** _____ amounts of gold, silver, and jewels. Where could these treasures be?

At times, the hunt seemed as **(4)** _____ as the original voyage. Time after time, the divers came up empty-handed. But Fisher had invested a lot of time and money in the project. He refused to give up the search.

Fisher was confident that one day, his crew would make their **(5)** _____ up to the surface with all the treasures from the *Atocha*. In 1975, one crew member found the best clue yet—nine cannons the ship had been carrying to protect itself from the **(6)** _____ pirate attacks. But Fisher and his crew were not able to find anything more at the time.

Write the Vocabulary Word that best completes the synonym web.

7.

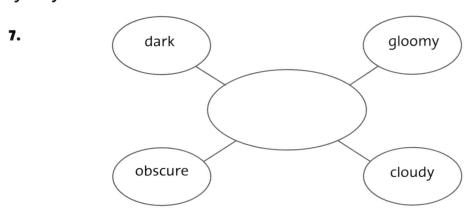

- dark
- gloomy
- obscure
- cloudy

Gold Beneath the Sea

by Linda Lott

The year was 1622, and it was an exciting time for brave adventurers. By then, the Spanish explorers knew that North America was filled with riches. Ships sailed back and forth across the sea endlessly, bringing goods from Spain to the new settlers in North America and leaving the continent loaded down with gold, silver, colorful gems, and lavish treasure. One of these ships was named *Nuestra Señora de Atocha*. **1**

Ships sailed back from North America loaded with treasures.

Stop and Think

1 Why was 1622 an exciting time for adventurers?

It was an exciting time because _____

_____

_____

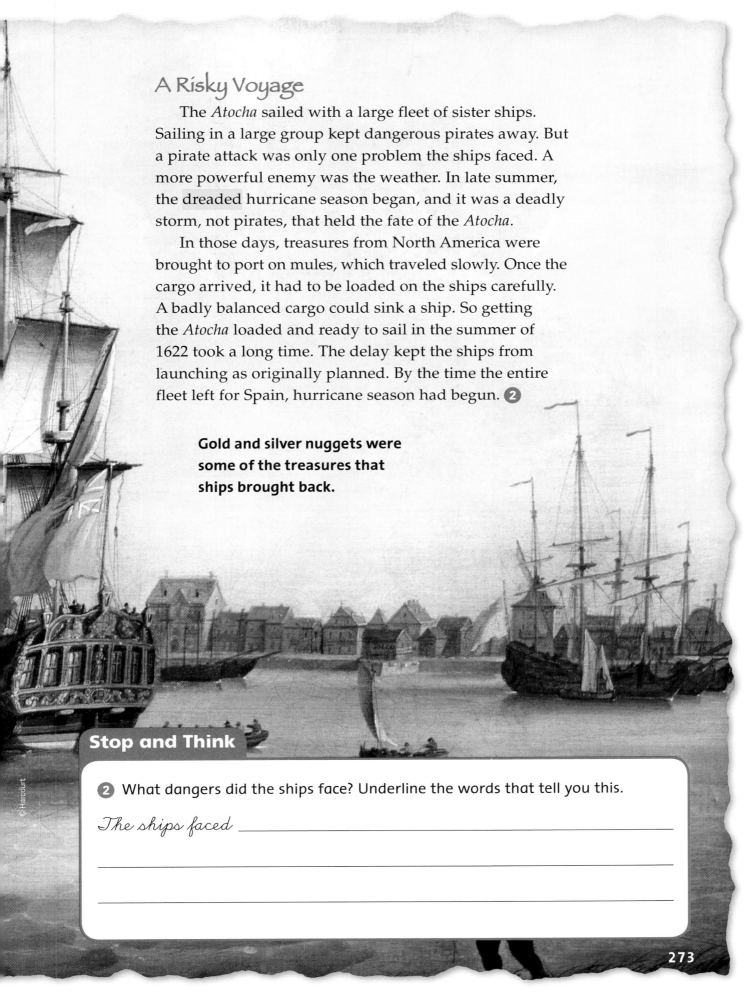

A Risky Voyage

The *Atocha* sailed with a large fleet of sister ships. Sailing in a large group kept dangerous pirates away. But a pirate attack was only one problem the ships faced. A more powerful enemy was the weather. In late summer, the dreaded hurricane season began, and it was a deadly storm, not pirates, that held the fate of the *Atocha*.

In those days, treasures from North America were brought to port on mules, which traveled slowly. Once the cargo arrived, it had to be loaded on the ships carefully. A badly balanced cargo could sink a ship. So getting the *Atocha* loaded and ready to sail in the summer of 1622 took a long time. The delay kept the ships from launching as originally planned. By the time the entire fleet left for Spain, hurricane season had begun. **2**

Gold and silver nuggets were some of the treasures that ships brought back.

Stop and Think

2 What dangers did the ships face? Underline the words that tell you this.

The ships faced _____

_____

_____

©Harcourt

The *Atocha* Is Lost

As the ships passed by what is now the state of Florida, a hurricane developed. The *Atocha*, traveling near the end of the line of ships, was doomed from the start. The ship's heavy cargo dragged it down 55 feet to the bottom of the sea. At the beginning of the trip, there were 265 sailors on board. Only five of them survived.

The traders were still hopeful that they could save the treasure, since they knew exactly where the *Atocha* had sunk. They tried again and again to reach the ship, but without modern equipment, the attempts failed. Then a new storm struck and hid the *Atocha's* remains.

The fleet sailed on, but the treasure was not forgotten. The Spanish tried to find the lost ship for many years, but the sea kept its secret. ❸

Hurricane season was a deadly time to sail.

© Harcourt

Stop and Think

❸ Why was the ship doomed from the start?

The ship was doomed from the start because _____

_____

_____

A Modern-Day Treasure Hunter

As a boy growing up in the 1930s in landlocked Indiana, Mel Fisher longed to be near the sea. He spent countless afternoons reading books about pirates and shipwrecks. He learned to swim and dive, and even made his own deep-sea diving suit to use when exploring a nearby lake.

When Fisher grew up, he went to California and started a dive shop. Along with his wife and partner Dolores, Fisher began diving for treasure off the California coast and elsewhere. After a few successes, they were hopelessly hooked on treasure hunting.

Searching for the *Atocha*

Fisher had known about the *Atocha* for years, and he thought he could find the lost ship. But first he had to invent some new equipment. Fisher created a useful device that he called the "mailbox." It shot out a powerful stream of clean water that swept away the sand and mud in dark, murky water. With this new device, divers could more easily find treasure scattered on the sea floor. **4**

Fisher's mailbox is a tube that is lowered over the boat's propellers.

Stop and Think

4 How does the mailbox help divers find treasure?

The mailbox _____

_____

_____

First Clue Is Found

In 1963, more than three hundred years after the *Atocha* sank, Fisher and his crew found 1,033 gold coins on the sea floor. Fisher exclaimed, "Once you have seen the ocean bottom paved with gold, you'll never forget it!"

They thought they were on the right track, but unfortunately the search wasn't over. In fact, it had barely begun. It was a long time before the divers found any more useful clues. Then, in 1975, one crew member found the best clue yet—nine cannons the ship had been carrying to protect itself from the dreaded pirate attacks.

Tragedy Strikes

The crew members were thrilled, but they didn't stay excited for long. Just a few days later, Dirk Fisher, Mel's oldest son, was in a boat with his wife and a diver. Tragically, the boat sank and all three aboard it died. It was a joyless crew that continued the search for the *Atocha* treasure. **5**

Fisher and his crew searched for the *Atocha* for sixteen years.

Stop and Think

5 Do you think Mel Fisher will find the treasure? Explain.

I think that _____

_____

_____

© Harcourt

Fisher and his crew found more than 40 tons of silver and gold.

Emeralds from the *Atocha*

A Silver Reef

Ten long years later, in July of 1985, one of the divers was exploring the sea off Key West, Florida. When the diver made his ascent back up to the ship and burst through the water's surface, everyone could tell that something exciting had occurred. The diver had uncovered a pile of silver bars on the bottom of the sea floor. Crew members at the time described the sight as a reef made of silver. Finally, all the hard work had paid off, and most of the *Atocha's* cargo had been found.

Now it was time to bring up treasures that hadn't seen the sun for hundreds of years, such as gold and silver coins, emeralds, gold chains, and other Spanish artifacts. Amazingly, the gold coins and bars were still somewhat shiny. **6**

Stop and Think

6 How could everyone tell that something exciting had occurred?

They could tell because _____

_____

_____

Who Gets the Treasure?

At first, both the state of Florida and the United States wanted a share of Fisher's long-sought treasure because it had been found in the coastal waters of the United States. Finally, the Supreme Court proclaimed that Fisher owned what he and his crew had found.

Fisher decided to sell some of the treasure and to place some of it in a museum. In the end, the search for the *Atocha* was successful as well as profitable.

Some people thought that Fisher might retire after that, but he continued to search for the remains of other lost ships. It wasn't the promise of riches that kept the treasure hunter searching, but the thrill of the search itself. **7**

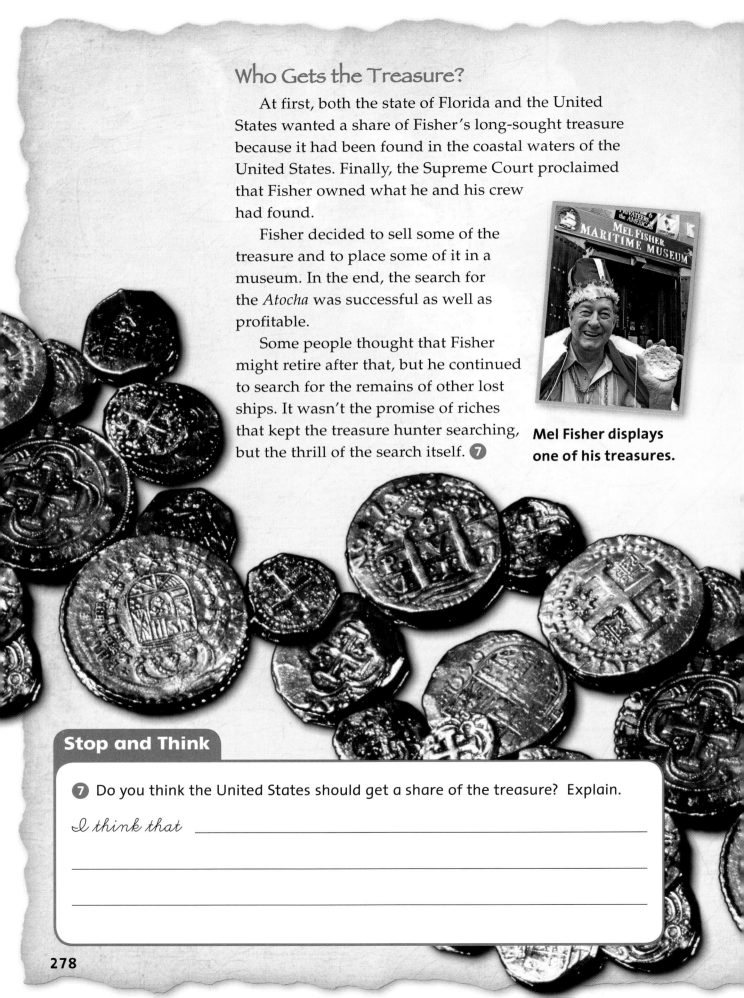

Mel Fisher displays one of his treasures.

Stop and Think

7 Do you think the United States should get a share of the treasure? Explain.

I think that _____

_____

_____

Think Critically

1. What did you learn about Mel Fisher's search for the *Atocha*?
Fill in the organizer with the main idea of the selection.
MAIN IDEA AND DETAILS

Detail	Detail	Detail
invented his own equipment	found gold coins in 1963	found the Atocha in 1985

Main Idea

2. What can you tell about Mel Fisher? How do you know this? CHARACTER

I can tell that _____

_____

_____

3. How does this selection make you feel? Explain your answer.
AUTHOR'S PURPOSE

This selection makes me feel _____

_____

_____

contemplate

contentedly

contrary

endanger

intolerable

officious

qualm

torrent

Vocabulary

Build Robust Vocabulary

Read the story and think about the meanings of the words in dark type.

It was the first day of school, and Alicia, Santha, and Tony stood **contentedly** at their bus stop, prepared for the yellow bus to stop at the curb. The doors slid open and they saw, **contrary** to every other day they had boarded a school bus, a metal box where the driver normally sat. The rest of the riders were looking slightly terrified.

"Step aboard," the voice from the box said in an **officious** tone. A sign on the side of the box said, *Due to an **intolerable** torrent of yelling aboard school buses, robotic drivers will bring students to and from school. Anyone who seeks to **endanger** this device will be reported to Principal Menendez.*

"Yikes!" said Santha. She had a **qualm** or two about letting a box drive her to school.

"Mr. Wu did look exhausted last spring," Tony exclaimed.

At the last stop, Scott was clearly shocked by the new bus driver. He stopped to **contemplate** the strange box, then rapped on the metal, calling out, "Mr. Wu? Are you in there?"

Write the answers to these questions. Use complete sentences. The first one has been done for you.

1. How did Alicia, Santha, and Tony feel as they stood **contentedly** at the bus stop?

   They felt pleased and satisfied with the way things were.

   _____

2. Why was the metal box **contrary** to what they had seen on the bus before?

   _____

   _____

3. What does an **officious** tone sound like?

   _____

   _____

4. What is an **intolerable torrent** of yelling?

   _____

   _____

5. If someone wanted to **endanger** a robotic device, what could they do?

   _____

   _____

6. Alicia had a **qualm** or two about having a robotic driver. What does this mean?

   _____

   _____

7. What was Scott doing when he stopped to **contemplate** the strange box?

   _____

   _____

© Harcourt

Box Driver

by David Neufeld

illustrated by Jeff Shelly

It was the first day of school, and Alicia, Santha, and Tony stood **contentedly** at their bus stop, prepared for the yellow bus to slow and then stop inches from the curb. The doors slid open and they saw, **contrary** to every other day they had boarded a school bus, a metal box where the driver normally sat. Then, an impersonal, robotic voice said, "Step aboard and find an empty seat." It volunteered in a computerized voice the number of seats that were empty, most of which were up front. The rest of the riders huddled in the back of the bus, peering out of the windows and looking slightly terrified. ❶

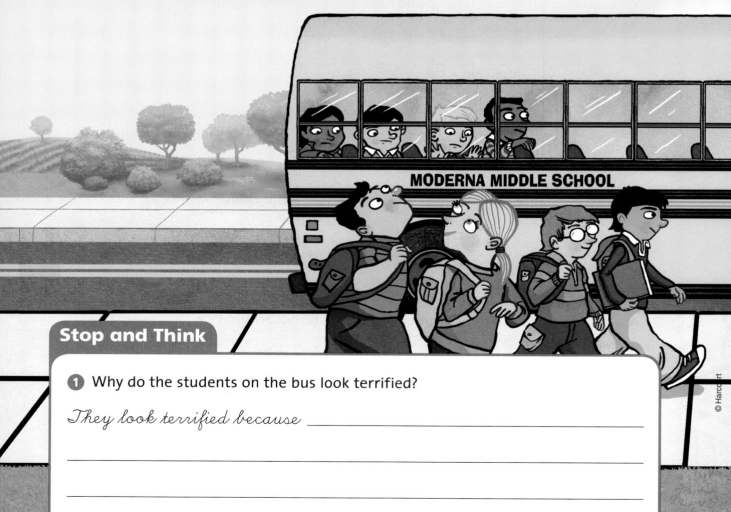

MODERNA MIDDLE SCHOOL

Stop and Think

❶ Why do the students on the bus look terrified?

They look terrified because _____

_____

_____

© Harcourt

Alicia paused at the bottom step of the bus, thinking this was some sort of gag. "Step aboard," the voice demanded again. A printed sign that was impossible to miss was located on the side of the box. It said, *Due to an intolerable torrent of yelling aboard school buses, robotic drivers will bring students to and from school. Anyone who seeks to endanger this device will be reported to Principal Menendez.*

"Yikes!" Santha said with a scowl. "I hope it knows how to drive." She didn't like computers as much as Alicia and Tony and had a qualm or two about letting a box made in a factory drive her to school.

"Mr. Wu did look exhausted last spring," Tony exclaimed, "and he was always telling us to be quiet." ②

Stop and Think

② What do you learn about Santha? Underline the words that tell you about her.

Santha _____

_____

_____

The three friends looked at each other, uncertain about this new development. With a shrug, Alicia climbed aboard and took her seat, with Santha following close behind her. Tony rolled his wheelchair onto a platform, and soon he was locked into his spot right behind the driver's box. "I can't see a thing," he grumbled with a frown.

"Every mechanical device is impersonal and impossible to predict," Santha said, clearly uneasy.

"So is my older brother," Alicia quipped, making the others giggle nervously.

The bus came to a safe stop at the next three corners. Scott, the last kid to get on, was clearly shocked by the new bus driver. He stopped to contemplate the strange box, then rapped on the metal, calling out, "Mr. Wu? Are you in there?" ❸

Stop and Think

❸ What do you think will happen next?

I think that _____

_____

_____

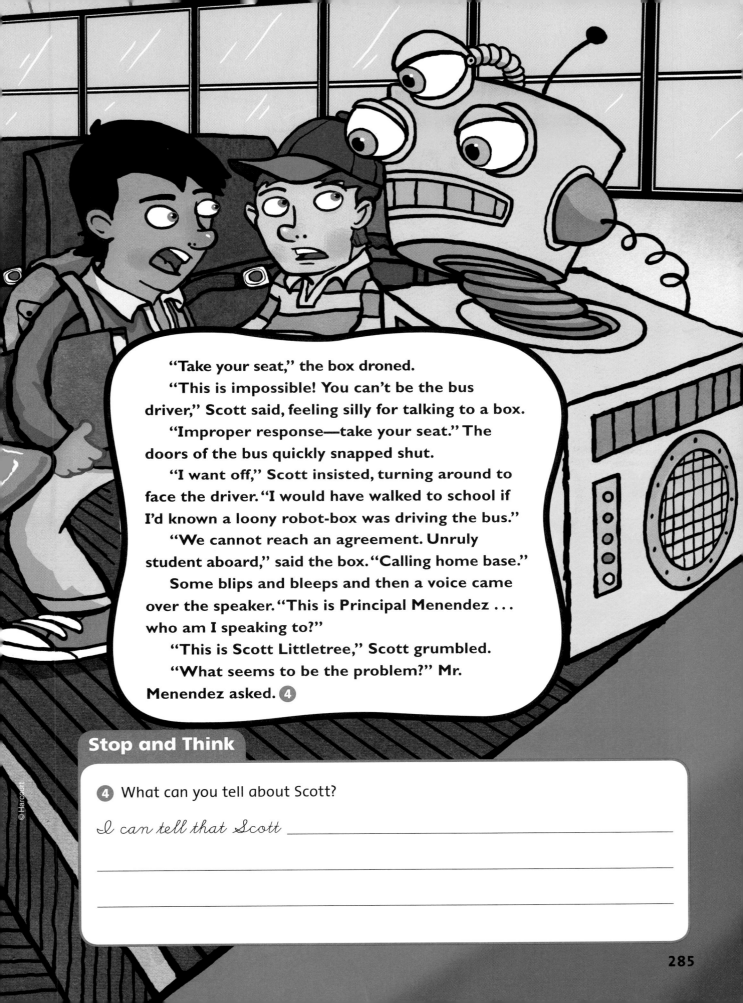

"Take your seat," the box droned.

"This is impossible! You can't be the bus driver," Scott said, feeling silly for talking to a box.

"Improper response—take your seat." The doors of the bus quickly snapped shut.

"I want off," Scott insisted, turning around to face the driver. "I would have walked to school if I'd known a loony robot-box was driving the bus."

"We cannot reach an agreement. Unruly student aboard," said the box. "Calling home base."

Some blips and bleeps and then a voice came over the speaker. "This is Principal Menendez . . . who am I speaking to?"

"This is Scott Littletree," Scott grumbled.

"What seems to be the problem?" Mr. Menendez asked. **4**

Stop and Think

4 What can you tell about Scott?

I can tell that Scott _____

_____

_____

"Why can't this box let me off?" Scott asked.

"Because I am pre-programmed to open only at specific stops," the robot replied, adding, "And I am not a box. I prefer the title of Principal Transporter."

Scott's eyes grew wide; the robot sounded indignant.

"That's certainly officious," said Mr. Menendez, "and I thought I was in charge here."

"No, I am in charge," the box stated forcefully.

"Oh, no," Mr. Menendez sighed, "I can see that this robot is imperfect. Students, sit tight—I'm on my way." **5**

Stop and Think

5 Why is the robot imperfect?

The robot is imperfect because _____

_____

_____

© Harcourt

286

Restless students roamed around the inside of the bus as they waited for Mr. Menendez to arrive. The doors wouldn't open and the windows seemed nailed shut.

"Take your seats . . . take your seats . . . take your seats," replied a nonending recording from the driver's seat.

Then, Tony spied a lever to the right of the box driver; the sign next to it said **PULL HERE IN EMERGENCY**. Tony pulled it and, finally, the doors swung open. The relieved students poured out, excitedly discussing the morning's events.

Moments later, Mr. Menendez arrived and took the lead of what became a short parade to the school. **6**

Stop and Think

6 How are the students freed from the bus?

The students are freed when _____

_____

_____

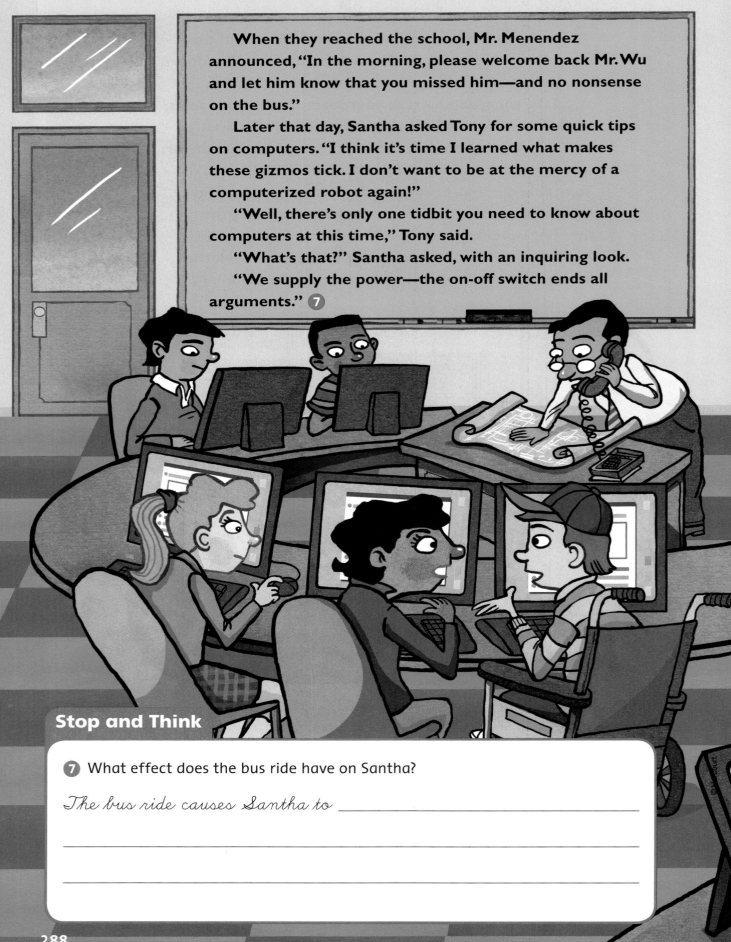

When they reached the school, Mr. Menendez announced, "In the morning, please welcome back Mr. Wu and let him know that you missed him—and no nonsense on the bus."

Later that day, Santha asked Tony for some quick tips on computers. "I think it's time I learned what makes these gizmos tick. I don't want to be at the mercy of a computerized robot again!"

"Well, there's only one tidbit you need to know about computers at this time," Tony said.

"What's that?" Santha asked, with an inquiring look.

"We supply the power—the on-off switch ends all arguments." **7**

Stop and Think

7 What effect does the bus ride have on Santha?

The bus ride causes Santha to _____

_____

_____

6. To say that Dr. Earle is brave would be a huge

_____ !

cacophony   torrent   understatement

7. Now under water, Dr. Earle looks for

_____ sea animals that

acute   erratic   elusive

few people have seen before.

8. The steady sound of Dr. Earle's breathing

_____ from the microphone

entrusts   emanates   implodes

inside the Jim Suit.

9. Everyone is surprised that they can't hear an

_____ heartbeat coming

erratic   elusive   unprecedented

from her microphone. Isn't she scared?

10. Dr. Earle says, "I don't feel as if I'm in any

_____ danger."

elusive   officious   acute

Write the answers to these questions. Use complete sentences.

11. What does Dr. Earle do that is unprecedented?

_____

_____

12. What is one piece of equipment that is critical to Dr. Earle during her dive?

_____

_____

A Daring Dive

by Gavin Light

CHARACTERS

NARRATOR   DR. SYLVIA EARLE
GRAHAM HAWKES   PHIL NEWTON
AL GIDDINGS   CHORUS

NARRATOR: It's September 19, 1979. Underwater explorer Sylvia Earle is about to entrust her life to a newly rediscovered device in underwater exploration: the Jim Suit.

CHORUS: The Jim Suit? What's that?

PHIL NEWTON: The Jim Suit is basically like an astronaut's space suit, only it's used underwater. My company, along with Graham Hawkes, redesigned a diving suit that was used by Jim Jarrett in 1935 when he explored the shipwrecked *Lusitania*.

AL GIDDINGS: Wait—I need to get some photos before we close the helmet of the suit. ❶

Stop and Think

❶ Why do you think the diving suit is named the "Jim Suit"?

I think that _____

_____

_____

GRAHAM HAWKES: It's critical that we make sure the air pressure is working correctly inside the suit. The air inside the suit must remain at the same pressure at all times. If it doesn't, the immense weight of the water above it could cause the suit to implode.

Al Giddings

CHORUS: We wouldn't want that to happen!

DR. EARLE: We've tested this suit so many times that I doubt anything will go wrong. Besides, I think driving on the freeway is more dangerous than this!

NARRATOR: The enormous helmet snaps shut, and Dr. Earle is lowered into the water.

GRAHAM HAWKES: Dr. Earle will be tethered by strap to a small submarine. After the sub tows her the 1,250 feet to the sea floor, it'll stay there until it's time to ascend to the surface.

AL GIDDINGS: I'm in the sub now, taking photographs of the entire unprecedented solo dive. We're descending into the ocean depths! ❷

Dr. Sylvia Earle and the Jim Suit

Stop and Think

❷ What can you tell about Dr. Earle? How can you tell?

I can tell that Dr. Earle _____

_____

_____

PHIL NEWTON: How are you doing, Dr. Earle? Do you see any elusive sea animals yet?

NARRATOR: The sound of Dr. Earle's breathing emanates from the microphone inside the Jim Suit.

DR. EARLE: No, not yet—I'm still descending.

AL GIDDINGS: We've reached the sea floor, and the colorful plants and animals are extraordinary! I'm taking some photos now. . . .

CHORUS: Click. . . Click. . . Click.

DR. EARLE: I'm walking on the sea floor, alone, and it's just breathtaking! But this suit is so cumbersome, I feel like a walking refrigerator. Right now, I'm stepping into a forest of bamboo coral. ③

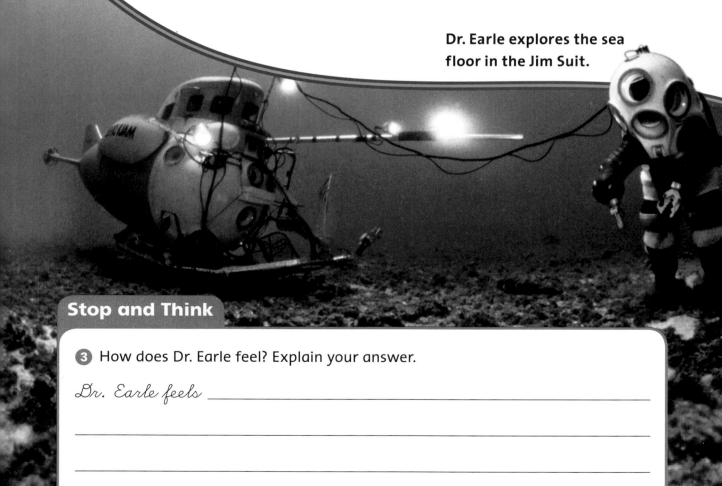

Dr. Earle explores the sea floor in the Jim Suit.

Stop and Think

③ How does Dr. Earle feel? Explain your answer.

Dr. Earle feels _____

_____

_____

Graham Hawkes: What does the bamboo coral look like, Dr. Earle?

Dr. Earle: They're long, white spirals, sort of like bed springs. They have black bands around them, and some of them are more than six feet tall.

Bamboo coral

Chorus: She's walking through *what?* A six-foot-tall coral forest?

Al Giddings: I can see flickering blue lights on the coral make an erratic blinking pattern when Dr. Earle brushes against it. The effect looks like blue flames.

Phil Newton: That must be the bioluminescence. At these great depths, the plants and animals often make their own light in order to scare away predators.

Dr. Earle: A great pale crab as big as a cat just paused to look at me. I doubt it's seen a strange jointed creature like me lumbering around on the sea floor before!

Swimming crab

Al Giddings: That's an understatement. That crab has definitely not seen anything remotely like a human before. **4**

Stop and Think

4 What causes the coral to blink?

The coral blinks because _____

_____

_____

305

Sandbar shark

DR. EARLE: Wait—I see a shark just ahead! Oh, it's just a small one, only about 18 inches long.

NARRATOR: Dr. Earle lumbers around slowly on the sea floor, hoping to glimpse an elusive sea creature.

DR. EARLE: I feel like I'm walking on the moon, but the moon isn't filled with all these life forms, such as bright red crabs and glowing fish. Oh—I just saw some lantern fish! They look like ocean liners gliding by with lighted windows!

CHORUS: Oooh! Cool fish!

PHIL NEWTON: Are you not just a bit fearful down there in the deep?

DR. EARLE: Oh, I don't feel as if I'm in any acute danger. I think we've planned well for any possible problems, and I entrust myself to you engineers up there! Safety is a matter of good teamwork. **5**

Lantern fish

Stop and Think

5 How might walking on the ocean floor feel like walking on the moon?

Walking on the ocean floor _____

_____

_____

Squid

NARRATOR: After exploring the sea floor for more than two hours, Dr. Earle begins her ascent to the surface. The sub slowly hauls her back to the waiting boat.

DR. EARLE: I really don't want to leave this fantastic environment. There must be a way to go even deeper into the sea. Why should we stop at 1,250 feet? The average depth of the sea is actually more than 13,000 feet! I want to go all the way to the very bottom.

GRAHAM HAWKES: I totally agree, Dr. Earle. More people have visited the moon than have explored the sea floor on our very own planet.

CHORUS: That's unbelievable!

NARRATOR: In a cacophony of clanging noises, Dr. Earle is raised up onto the boat.

AL GIDDINGS: That was awesome! **6**

Stop and Think

6 Do you think Dr. Earle will continue to make deep-sea dives? How can you tell?

I think Dr. Earle _____

_____

_____

© Harcourt

Dr. Earle shakes hands with Graham Hawkes.

PHIL NEWTON: I think we should call you "Her Deepness" now, Dr. Earle. You've just become the first person to walk on the sea floor without being connected to the surface.

CHORUS: Her Deepness . . . we like it!

GRAHAM HAWKES: Actually, two men have gone deeper than this, but they lasted only twenty minutes on the sea floor before abandoning the mission. It was too dangerous.

DR. EARLE: Oh, yes, I read all about Jacques Piccard and Don Walsh's trip into the deep in 1960. If they can accomplish that, then surely we can achieve it, too.

NARRATOR: Now, this one journey into the deep is over, but Dr. Earle's search for even better technology is just beginning. After this dive, Dr. Earle and Graham Hawkes went on to create the Deep Rover, a submersible that can be operated on the sea floor. With this new technology, Dr. Earle still hopes to explore the very depths of the sea. **7**

Stop and Think

7 Do you think "Her Deepness" is a good nickname for Dr. Earle? Explain.

I think "Her Deepness" _____

_____

_____

Think Critically

1. Why did Dr. Earle dive to the sea floor? MAIN IDEA AND DETAILS

Dr. Earle dived to the sea floor because _____

_____

_____

2. How does this selection make you feel about exploring the ocean? AUTHOR'S PURPOSE

This selection makes me feel _____

_____

_____

3. Do you think the sea floor should be explored? Explain.
MAKE JUDGMENTS

I think the sea floor _____

_____

_____

_____

_____

_____

Lesson 22
220 (b) Jean Clottes/Associated Press; 220 (t) PhotoEdit/PhotoEdit; 221 (tr) PhotoEdit/ PhotoEdit; 221 (b) Sisse Brimberg/National Geographic/Getty Images; 222 Sisse Brimberg/National Geographic/Getty Images; 224 (t) Hemis/Alamy; 224 Sisse Brimberg/ National Geographic/Getty Images; 225 (br) Serge de Sazo/Photo Researchers, Inc.; 226 Jean Clottes/Associated Press; 228 PhotoEdit/PhotoEdit

Lesson 24
230 (t) Sisse Brimberg/National Geographic/Getty Images; 240 (bg) Chris Rennie/ Getty Images; 240 (cr) Michael Freeman/Digital Vision/Getty Images; 241 (b) John Van Hasselt/Corbis Sygma; 242 (bg) Chris Rennie/Getty Images; 242 Panoramic Images/Getty Images; 243 (inset) Michael Freeman/Digital Vision/Getty Images; 244 (bg) Chris Rennie/ Getty Images; 244 Wolfgang Kaehler/Corbis; 246 (bg) Chris Rennie/Getty Images; 247 Wolfgang Kaehler/Corbis; 248 (bg) Chris Rennie/Getty Images; 248 (bg) David Madison/ Getty Images; 248 (c) John Van Hasselt/Corbis Sygma

Lesson 25
250 (t) Jeremy Woodhouse/Digital Vision/Getty Images; 254 Barry Cronin/ZUMA/Corbis; 255 (inset) Franco Pizzochero/AGE Fototstock; 256 Jorg Muller/Alamy; 257 (inset) Marc Hill/Alamy; 258 Jeremy Woodhouse/Digital Vision/Getty Images; 259 (inset) Geogphotos/Alamy

Lesson 26
260 (bg) ImageState/Alamy; 260 (c) NASA/Roger Ressmeyer/CORBIS; 261 (br) Woodmansterne/Topham/The Image Works; 262 ImageState/Alamy; 262 (c) NASA/Roger Ressmeyer/CORBIS; 264 (I) Bettmann/CORBIS; 264 (bg) NASA/Photo Researchers, Inc.; 265 (b) Handout/Reuters/Corbis; 266 Roger Harris/Photo Researchers, Inc.; 268 (bg) Charles O'Rear/CORBIS; 269 (br) Woodmansterne/Topham/The Image Works

Lesson 27
270 (t) Jonathan Blair - Woodfin Camp; 270 (b) Thomas Mellish/The Bridgeman Art Library/Getty Images; 271 (b) Courtesy of Mel Fisher's Treasures; 272 (r) AP Photo/Bureau of Immigration and Customs Enforcement; 272 (I) Jonathan Blair/CORBIS; 272 (bg) Thomas Mellish/The Bridgeman Art Library/Getty Images; 274 (bg) The Art Archive/ Rasmus Mayer Coll, Bergen/Dagli Orti (A); 275 (t) Courtesy of Mel Fisher's Treasures; 275 (b) Courtesy of Mel Fisher's Treasures; 276 Courtesy of Mel Fisher's Treasures; 277 (t) Johnathan Blair/Corbis; 277 (inset) VICTOR R. BOSWELL, JR/National Geographic; 278 (tr) Bob Krist/Corbis; 278 (b) Jonathan Blair - Woodfin Camp; 278 (bg) Thomas Mellish/The Bridgeman Art Gallery/Getty Images

Lesson 30
300 (cr) Al Giddings/Al Giddings Images, Inc.; 300 (br) Charles Nicklin/Al Giddings Images, Inc.; 300 (bg) SAS/Alamy; 301 (cr) Charles Nicklin/Al Giddings Images, Inc.; 301 (tr) Masa Ushioda/ V&W/Bruce Coleman, Inc.; 302 Charles Nicklin/Al Giddings Images, Inc.; 302 (bg) SAS/Alamy; 303 (c) Al Giddings/Al Giddings Images, Inc.; 303 (tr) Rosemary Chastney/Al Giddings Images, Inc.; 304 (b) Charles Nicklin/Al Giddings Images, Inc.; 304 (bg) SAS/Alamy; 305 (br) Masa Ushioda/V&W/Bruce Coleman, Inc.; 305 (tr) Photo by Woods Hole Oceanograqhic Institution; 306 (t) David Fleetham/Alamy; 306 (cr) Doc White/Nature Picture Library; 306 (bg) SAS/ Alamy; 307 (t) Al Giddings/Al Giddings Images, Inc.; 308 (tr) Don Howard/NOAA; 308 (bg) SAS/Alamy; 309 (tr) Geri Murphy; BrandX,Royalty Free/Robertstock